KAI JAINA: A WORLD BETWEEN
A MEMOIR

BY
JOE BANIVANUA MAR

Grosvenor House
Publishing Limited

The right of Joe Banivanua Mar to be identified as the author of this
work has been asserted in accordance with Section 78
of the Copyright, Designs and Patents Act 1988

This book is published by
Grosvenor House Publishing Ltd
Link House
140 The Broadway, Tolworth, Surrey, KT6 7HT.
www.grosvenorhousepublishing.co.uk

A CIP record for this book
is available from the British Library

Paperback ISBN 978-1-83615-179-1
Hardback ISBN 978-1-83615-180-7
eBook ISBN 978-1-83615-181-4

To those who shaped my journey

To my mother, whose many sacrifices gave me the start I needed and who never lived to see the dreams she held for her son fulfilled.

To my father, who I was too young to know and whose stories I never got to hear.

To my sister, Sera, whose drive for us to pursue our education was unrelenting.

To my daughter Tracey, who first encouraged me to write these memoirs and left us far too soon, on the cusp of her fullest potential.

And to those who walk with me still: my wife and soulmate for the last forty years, Sarah, my beloved daughters, Sera and Lina, and my grandchildren Nisi, Jimmy and Monty (Yaca)—my love for you all runs deep.

ABOUT THE BOOK

KAI JAINA: A WORLD BETWEEN

In this deeply personal and inspiring memoir, **Josaia Mar** takes readers on a remarkable journey across continents, cultures and moments of profound transformation. Born in a remote Fijian village, he shares his rise to leadership in the global corporate world while navigating the challenges of family, identity and faith.

From his humble beginnings as a curious boy in Fiji to becoming a champion of ethical governance and cultural harmony, this memoir reflects on love, loss and the pursuit of purpose. He also delves into the complexities of raising children in a multicultural family from, overcoming misunderstandings to nurturing a sense of belonging in children of mixed heritage.

Through coups, career triumphs and the heartbreak of losing a child, he emerges as a man of resilience and hope, bound by the unbreakable ties of heritage and family.

Kai Jaina: A World Between is a story of courage, connection and the enduring power of dreams. It is a celebration of life's challenges and triumphs, woven with a voice as warm and welcoming as a fireside chat.

Acknowledgements

I extend my heartfelt gratitude to the many people who have, in their own way, contributed to the completion of this book.

To Sarah, Jill, Ratu Isoa Gavidi and Richard Naidu—your suggestions, corrections and shared memories have helped shape this narrative.

To Jesoni Vitusagavulu, whose relentless reminders and persistent question, "When will the book be finished?" provided the gentle yet firm nudge I needed to bring it to completion.

To my dearest daughter, Tracey, whose early advice to include personal stories I wholeheartedly embraced in crafting this memoir. Though you are no longer here to see the finished product, I hope it reflects the spirit of what you envisioned and that you would be proud of it.

Finally, to my dearest wife, Sarah and to my other beloved daughters, Sera and Lina, whose unwavering belief in my ability to write this book has been a source of strength and motivation. Your love and faith have carried me through.

Thank you all for being part of this journey.

CONTENTS

INTRODUCTION: IN SEARCH OF LOST STORIES

To my three daughters and grandchildren,

I never truly realised the weight of lost stories until I began searching for traces of your grandfather and great-grandfather. What I thought would be a simple task—piecing together the life of the man who gave me half of mine—turned out to be a journey filled with frustration, silence and occasional despair. The truth is the past slips away easily when it is not written down. Our people, the indigenous Fijians, have always been storytellers, passing down history through word of mouth. But oral histories, though rich, are often victims of time. They stretch, they fade and they change. And the details of one man's life—like my father's—can disappear into the haze of memory, leaving only fragments behind.

Your grandfather, my father, was one of those fragments. A Chinese shopkeeper in a remote Fijian village, he died when I was just two years old. He remains a stranger to me, and much of what I know about him is as fragile as the few faint recollections I have. I remember a tall, almost ghostly figure, his white clothing shimmering as he emerged from the copra drying shed, a pith hat casting a shadow across his face. It is one of the few memories I have, one that I can almost touch but never truly grasp, and it is one I have clung to desperately.

What haunts me the most, though, is not the lack of written history, but my own denial. Growing up in the village, where ignorance about other cultures bred prejudice, children, particularly from the other villages, taunted me for being different—for being half Chinese. The words *kai jaina* (person from China) became a label, a wound and a brand of shame. It was not just the other children's teasing that stung; it was the internal shame, the rejection of a part of myself that I could not erase. For years, I tried to hide my Chineseness, denying who I was to escape the cruelty of my peers. In doing so, I turned my back on my father's legacy, on the stories I could have learned had I not been too young or had I been brave enough to ask, when there were still people to tell them.

Now, I carry that regret. The people who knew him, the ones who could have told me about his life, are long gone. I am left with this emptiness, this hole where his story should be. I wish I had known then what I know now—that to understand ourselves, we must embrace every part of where we come from, even the parts we want to forget.

I write this memoir for you, my children and grandchildren, not only as a record of my own life but as a way to preserve the stories that define us. My hope is that, through these pages, you find both the roots that ground you and the wings that carry you forward.

Some of these may be difficult for you to read as they were difficult for me to admit, and I ask myself—am I being too hard on myself? On balance, I do not think

I am. But I do not want you to think that I carry a burden or bitterness—I have made peace with my past. In fact, the pain and the regret sit side by side with the many joyful memories of the village and of all of you. Am I sounding too serious and gloomy? Do not be fooled. There is a deep, mischievous sense of humour I was born with, and I know each of you have been on the receiving end of it more than once. I hope that humour transcends this period of retrospection and comes through in the later chapters. There are many lighter moments, just as there are moments of reflection.

But I am getting ahead of myself. Let me take you back to the beginning.

CHAPTER 1

THE FAMILY—ROOTS OF RESILIENCE

I was born on 28 August 1945 in Naroi village, just before the end of the Second World War, on the island of Moala, one of the 300 islands that made up Fiji. Moala is a small dot in the Pacific, only about 24 square miles, lying 100 nautical miles southeast of Suva, Fiji's capital. It is a place of quiet shores, swaying coconut trees and a timeless rhythm that had been undisturbed for generations. Yet, despite its serenity, my arrival into this world was anything but simple.

My parents came from two vastly different worlds. My mother, Akenisi Moceikete, was a native Fijian, born and raised on Moala. Her roots ran deep within the land, as a member of the Nakoroicake clan, part of the Nasau tribe, who had called this island home for centuries. My father, Mar Kim Qun, was a stranger to these shores. He arrived in Fiji from mainland China in the early 1930s, seeking a new life. Eventually, he made his way to Moala and settled in the village of Naroi, where he established a small trade store—one of only two stores serving the village's modest population of about 200 people.

Their union was never formalised by marriage, yet together they created a family in this remote corner of the world. My siblings—my brother George, my sister

Sisi and I—were born into a mix of cultures, a blend of Chinese and Fijian. It should have been a celebration of diversity, but in reality it made us outsiders in both worlds.

For indigenous Fijians, identity was rooted in the *vanua*—the land—and in the unbroken traditions passed down from generation to generation. Each Fijian belonged to a *yavusa* (tribe), which connected them to the land and gave them certain rights passed down through patriarchal lines. We had no such claim. Our father was a Chinese man, an outsider, and so we, his children, lived at the margins of tradition. Despite living and breathing the Fijian way of life, and despite fulfilling every traditional responsibility expected of us, we were excluded from the registry of indigenous Fijians—the *i Vola ni Kawa Bula*. We grew up as if we were part of the community, but in the eyes of the law and tradition, we were something else. Not fully Fijian. Not fully Chinese. Just... different.

For many years, this duality shaped our identity in subtle yet profound ways. To the Fijians, we were outsiders trying to blend in; to the Chinese, we were family yet unfamiliar, shaped by a culture they did not understand. These blurred boundaries became both a challenge and a gift: a challenge in navigating acceptance and belonging, yet a gift in offering us the opportunity to see and appreciate life through multiple lenses.

It was not until 1985, decades later and only after repeated representations by myself and Ratu Nacanieli Draunidalo (the island's Chief and my brother-in-law), that we were finally recognised by the Fijian government and admitted into the registry. Only then did we and our children gain the right to call ourselves Fijian, to claim the heritage that had been denied to us for so long. It was a bittersweet victory, arriving too late to change the years we spent as strangers in our own land, but thankfully not too late to claim our rights in the land that shaped us.

Reflecting on those early days, I cannot help but feel the weight of what was lost: my father's quiet presence—his foreignness in a village that saw him as different—and the way that difference rippled through our lives, creating an invisible wall that kept us on the fringes. I wonder now about the stories he might have told, about the wisdom of his homeland that I might have absorbed, had I not been too young or brave enough to ask, and too ashamed to listen. Those questions linger, unanswered and irretrievable, another reminder of how shame can silence even the strongest of family bonds.

Our family, however, was much larger than just my parents, George, Sisi and I. My mother's first husband, Jone, had died, leaving her with three surviving children—two boys, Kata and Jone, and a girl, Sera. A fourth boy, Biu, had passed away at an early age. After my father died, my mother remarried and had two more boys, Tevita and Cakacaka. In Fiji, half-brothers and half-sisters are always treated as full siblings, and so, with the surviving children, eventually, we were a happy family of eight siblings.

My mother was a gentle, wonderful person who taught us strong ethical values, a deep sense of independence and, most importantly, the importance of family bonds—unsurprisingly, given her own experiences. I have many fond memories of her, but perhaps the sweetest is the recollection of sleeping next to her as a child, the softness of her arm my pillow, her warmth a shield against the night's cold and her love my comfort. Even now, as I close my eyes, I can feel the soft warmth of those moments.

When we lost our mother, it was as though the very foundation of our family shifted. My eldest brother Kata naturally assumed the role of patriarch. A man of few words, he embodied the teachings of the Baha'i Faith, which I later came to embrace—"Let deeds, not words, be your adorning." His quiet confidence became a steady anchor for us all. He was wise in traditional matters but open to seeking advice on the challenges of the modern world. As the *turaga ni koro* (village headman), he was respected for his wisdom and sound judgment. Kata's quiet confidence made him a guiding force in the village, a role he accepted with grace and humility.

Sera, my eldest sister, became the matriarch upon our mother's passing. She was the driving force behind ensuring that her younger siblings received a good education. Relentless in her ambition for us, she enlisted the help of her husband, Ratu Nacanieli Draunidalo, who was my teacher at the village school and later became the village and island chief after his father's death. Sera's determination paved the way for the future success of myself and our younger brothers, and we owe so much to her unwavering belief in the importance of education. Sera and Sisi, as was the custom of the times were not encouraged by our parents to pursue further education but to remain home with our mother. This was a tremendous waste of opportunity and talent as my sisters had wisdom and abilities that could have been used far beyond the confines of the village.

Now, at the age of 79, I find myself reflecting on these memories with a sense of timelessness and nostalgic sadness. One by one, my siblings and our parents have passed on, and I remain the last of our mother's nine children. There is a quiet loneliness in being the final link to a generation that is no more. The house once filled with the noise and laughter of my family is now a memory, but those bonds remain deeply etched in my heart.

Chapter 2

Village life—where the sea meets the hills

Naroi is a village cradled between the sea and the hills, where life moved with the tides and seasons. Nestled along a one kilometre stretch of beach, it was sheltered by two rocky headlands and a fringing reef that softened the Pacific Ocean's waves. The village extended about 200 metres inland, gently rising up hills that shielded us from the winds. This was my world—self-contained, supported by the land and sea.

Growing up, we had little need for commercial goods. The sea teemed with fish, and the rich volcanic soil gave life to root crops and tropical vegetables that sustained us. Saving for the future, whether in money or possessions, felt like trying to store the ocean tide. It was a foreign concept. For us, life was immediate, sustained by what we could grow or gather that day. There was an unspoken wisdom in this way of life—its rhythm and simplicity left little room for the complexities of the outside world.

Our homes were *bures,* traditional thatched huts made from coconut and pandanus trees: simple one-room structures with sand-covered floors and woven palm walls. Families shared this space, separated only by a thin curtain dividing the parents' sleeping area from the rest of the house, which served as both the dining and sleeping quarters for the children. Everyone slept on the floor on hand woven straw mats. A small lean-to outside functioned as the kitchen, where meals were cooked over an open fire.

But change was creeping into our village. The outside world became harder to ignore. The arrival of white settlers and missionaries in the late 1800s and early 1900s brought the concept of money. Along with their ships came goods we had never needed before—clothes, kerosene for lamps, sugar and salt to flavour our food and soap for washing. These items could not be bartered for; they required money, a currency that slowly seeped into our daily lives.

For a while, copra—the dried meat of coconuts— became our main source of cash. Coconut trees were plentiful on the island, and copra was in demand for making oil. We dried and bagged the copra and sent it on by coastal cutters to Suva, receiving a modest amount of money in return. It was not much, but enough to purchase the few items the changing world demanded.

Our *bures* slowly gave way to wooden or concrete houses, more permanent structures that promised security but somehow lacked the warmth of our thatched homes. Yet, in many ways, our lives stayed tied to the land and sea, a simple economy that remained steady as long as we planted enough crops and caught enough fish. The shift was subtle but profound, though. While the core of village life persisted, these small changes hinted at the broader transformations waiting beyond the horizon.

Despite these encroaching changes, many aspects of life remained communal. Rebuilding a house, for instance, was a village affair. The tasks were divided by the chief or headman, and the entire community would come together to help. But as modern goods became more essential, the need for cash grew. Copra increasingly became our link to the outside world, funding the small luxuries that marked progress and enabling some form of commerce to take hold.

Life in those days was hard but also idyllic. We rose with the sun—or with the crowing of roosters—and followed a steady routine. For breakfast, we boiled *drauni moli* (lemon leaves) tea and ate what the land provided: root crops (cassava, taro or yam) or, on rare occasions when flour was available, thin pancakes. The early mornings during mango season are etched in my memory, racing through darkness to beat the other children to the mango bushes, our hands sticky with juice before the village had even stirred.

School was simple, with barefoot children dressed in hand-me-down clothes. Boys went bare-chested in shorts or *sulus* (lap laps), while the girls wore second-, third- or even fourth-hand dresses. With soap scarce, we wore these clothes for days. The school building was a single room, and lessons were basic writing, reading and arithmetic, taught in Fijian. English was a curiosity to us, taught from a book about farm animals that we had never seen.

Most of our learning, however, happened outside. The land was our first teacher, offering lessons in fishing, farming and the natural rhythms of the island and the seasons. Each task taught us about patience, resilience and respect for the world around us. After school, we changed into work clothes and helped with daily tasks—gathering coconuts, weeding food gardens or collecting firewood. These chores, though demanding, were part of the tapestry of our lives, blending responsibility with the joys of youth.

Evenings were a communal affair. We bathed in the village brook, which split into two tributaries—one for men, the other for women. Soap was too precious to waste on washing, so we used rough, flat stones to scrub ourselves clean. Afterwards, we warmed ourselves by the fire, the smell of burning wood mingling with the scent of dinner cooking nearby. Dinner often consisted of fish and taro leaves cooked in fresh coconut cream, accompanied by root vegetables like cassava or *uvi* (yam). This was followed by more *drauni moli* tea.

After dinner, the village settled down, often to traditional singing with the gentle strumming of a guitar or the soft hum of hymns that filled the night air, our voices lifting in harmony—a ritual that, I believe, helped cultivate the musical talent Fijians are known for today. On other nights, the adults gathered for *kava*, a mildly narcotic drink made from the *yagona* root. For us children, it was time for games until the dreaded village drum, a signal that punctuated our lives, sounded at nine o'clock, marking bedtime.

Many of the village rules were rooted in the Christian faith brought by the missionaries. Even the names of the days represented what work was prescribed for the day. Sundays were *Siga Tabu* (taboo day), sacred days when no work or play was allowed. Fridays were *Vakaraubuka* (firewood preparation) and Saturdays *Vakarauwai* (water preparation).

Methodism, with its strict rules, shaped the rhythm of our lives. We learned early to respect Sunday's rules: no playing, no lying, no killing animals. It was more than just obedience to rules; it was our way of honouring something beyond ourselves, even when we were too young to understand it fully. The threat of eternal punishment for breaking these rules was drilled into us, instilling a deep obedience to the faith.

Fridays and Saturdays became joyful days—collecting firewood and fetching water to prepare for the Sunday's feast, which was cooked in underground ovens called *lovos*. These rituals, though modest, bound us as a family and a community as the tasks, while necessary, were family-based, creating opportunities for bonding and fun as we worked together. It was a weekly reminder of the importance of family cohesion. Sundays also gave children a rare chance to stay up past the nine o'clock curfew, if the evening church service ran long—although I dreaded this, knowing it usually meant enduring a lengthy sermon.

Despite the strict rules, we found joy in the freedom village life offered. After dinner, if we were not caught by the drum, we played games like hide-and-seek. The rush to get home before curfew became an adventure. I remember one night, running back after the nine o'clock drum, misjudging the height of a wooden house's floor and knocking myself out cold. Worse still, I got caught and received three strokes of the cane from the headmaster the next Monday. We laughed about it later, but at the time, the headmaster's cane was no laughing matter.

Life in the village was hard, but it was rich with joy and community. We made up for what we lacked in wealth in shared laughter and the bonds that tied us together. It was a place where even the smallest changes—like a new piece of clothing from a visiting Indian trader or a new tool from a passing boat—became events. The village had a way of turning the ordinary into the extraordinary, and those vivid memories remain with me to this day.

CHAPTER 3

SWEET MOMENTS AND HIDDEN JOYS

For young boys one of the most exciting activities after Sunday school was making sweets, or *loli*, as we called them. It was a forbidden joy, a secret adventure that bonded us. Each of us contributed something—sugar sneakily taken from home, lemons gathered the day before, or fresh coconut cream we made just for the occasion. The last and most critical ingredient was finding someone's kitchen that was not being used, preferably one out of sight. This ensured we did not have to share our carefully crafted sweets with prying siblings or curious adults.

The process of making these sweets was simple but to us then, it was magical. We would heat the sugar in a saucepan, waiting for it to melt just enough, then quickly squeeze in the lemon juice. The coconut cream followed, stirred in gently. Timing was everything—we had to be careful not to overcook the sugar. Once the mixture reached just the right consistency, we would quickly scoop it into dollops and drop them into a basin of water, watching as they hardened into lemon-flavoured coconut cream lollies. To this day, the taste lingers in my memory—a rich, tangy sweetness that carried with it the essence of carefree childhood, fleeting yet unforgettable.

The girls in our village had their own special activities too. Sometimes they would join us in hide-and-seek or swimming on the beach, but more often they spent time learning essential skills from the older women. Fishing, prawning and cooking were a big part of their days, as was learning to weave mats and baskets. They even made us hats as gifts, each one woven with care, each one a token of love and community. Looking back, I realise how much richness those activities added to our lives—innocent fun woven into the very fabric of our cultural heritage. We did not rely on manufactured games or artificial distractions like today's instant-gratification culture. We thrived on creativity and resourcefulness. Everything we used came from the land, which grounded us in a way that feels rare now.

Tuesday nights were always special in the village—it was radio session night. Nearly everyone gathered in the chief's house to listen to one of the two radios in the village: the other belonged to the island's medical officer. Those nights felt magical; the radio crackled to life, filling the room with voices and music that carried us beyond the island into a world of mystery and marvel. To my young mind, the idea of voices and melodies emerging from that mysterious box was nothing short of miraculous. I imagined tiny people living inside the radio, speaking, singing and playing guitar. The thought seemed perfectly logical back then, a child's attempt to make sense of the wondrous unknown.

On rare occasions, a *kai palagi*—a European— would visit the island. This was an event of great significance, one that brought both curiosity and reverence. Fiji was still a British colony, and top government positions were held by British administrators, including the District

Commissioner (DC), who oversaw the eastern part of the Fiji Islands (the provinces of Lomaiviti and Lau, which includes Moala). His visits, though infrequent, perhaps once every two years, were momentous. To our young minds, the DC was not just a government figure; he was a mythical presence whose arrival transformed our quiet island into a bustling hub of activity.

In Fijian culture, you do not treat chiefs as your equals unless you are of a similar rank. Respect and subservience were ingrained in us from a young age. You did not dare look them in the eye, and if you crossed paths with them, you stepped aside, sat down and clapped your hands in reverence—*cobo*—until they passed. The DC was treated with this same level of deference.

Whenever the DC visited, the entire island of Moala would be mobilised to prepare for a *soqo levu*—a grand ceremony. The preparation began days in advance, and the air buzzed with excitement and urgency. The DC was accorded the highest honours, even from the moment he arrived. It felt as though the entire village held its breath, awaiting his arrival with reverence, each of us ready to play our part. A special platform with an armchair for him would be built, and he would be carried ashore by a group of young men on this chair perched on top of the platform, a symbolic gesture that set the tone for the whole event.

As children, we were kept at a distance. The adults did not trust us to maintain the required reverence, so our only way to catch a glimpse of this 'minor god' was by sneaking peeks through the woven reeds of the *bure* walls. To us, the DC appeared in pristine white, with his pith hat adorned with feathers, a figure out of another world, almost ethereal—especially to our wide-eyed, young minds. He seemed untouchable, a symbol of authority that, even as children, we instinctively respected.

Growing up, this deference extended to all *kai palagis*. We were taught to address them with titles—Mr, Miss or Mrs—never by their first names. To do otherwise was a sign of disrespect and over-familiarity. This deference became so deeply ingrained that even when I rose to a senior position in Shell Pacific Islands Ltd company, I struggled to call my boss by his first name, despite him urging me to. It took me two years to finally call him 'Tom' instead of 'Mr Millard.'

The *soqo levu* for the DC would often last several hours, with various traditional presentations before any official government business was conducted. These included the *i sevusevu* (offering of yaqona), the *i qaloqalovi* (ceremonial welcome) and the *magiti vakaturaga* (chiefly feast), along with traditional dances like the *vakamalolo* (sitting down dance), *meke wesi* (spear dance), *meke i wau* (war club dance) and the *lakalaka* (story dramatisation dance). Of course, no ceremony would be complete without the DC partaking in several bowls of *yaqona*—the traditional *kava* drink. I often wondered what he thought of these protocols, particularly after drinking bowl after bowl of *yaqona*, which is an acquired taste to say the least! No wonder his visits were so few and far between.

Life in the village was shaped by moments like these— simple joys, shared adventures and occasional brush with the extraordinary. They were threads woven together and leaving memories, though fleeting, that are etched in my heart.

CHAPTER 4

VILLAGE SCHOOL AND LESSONS
BEYOND THE CLASSROOM

All too soon, the carefree days of playing in the sun came to an abrupt halt as we entered the world of school. The endless tropical days filled with freedom were replaced by the regimented structure of education—a world that seemed far less inviting to a young boy like me. It was a transition from boundless curiosity to the confines of lessons and rules, yet one that would shape the course of my life.

Our primary school was shared between two villages, Naroi and Vunuku. There was just one teacher, and the school went up to class five. There were about fifty of us, from class one at age five to class five at about age ten. Our 'school' was the village church. With no pencils or paper, we adapted to what we had, using small cowrie shells from the beach to form letters on the church floor, arranging them with care and precision. It was simple yet demanding, and each time we carefully arranged those small shells into letters, I felt a growing appreciation for this mysterious world of knowledge that seemed to be transforming the ordinary into something meaningful.

Looking back, it often puzzled me how so much effort and the village's scarce resources were poured into building churches while education took a back seat. Each village had its own church, the grandest and most prominent structure around, yet we had to make do with a makeshift school and little in the way of materials. It was a contradiction—a desire to honour our faith through imposing structures but not through the education that could deepen that faith. This contradiction stayed with me well into adulthood, influencing the way I saw the priorities of the world around me.

Finally, in 1953, my prayers were answered. A proper wooden school building was constructed, and a traditional *bure* was built as a second building by the villagers. With this, another teacher was appointed, and we were introduced to writing slates—a huge leap forward in my young mind. The smooth slate under my hand felt like a portal, each scratch of chalk a mark on a future that seemed just a little more possible with each line. By my final year, we even had pencils and paper, a luxury that felt nothing short of miraculous.

The first and only English book we had was used for our reading lessons. It was called *Farmer Joe,* and the name sticks with me to this day. The book introduced us to strange and exotic animals we had never seen—cows, sheep, elephants and even lions and tigers. In our imaginations, these creatures, although distant and foreign, came alive. Their strange forms were etched into our memories by the vivid descriptions and crude illustrations. Those images fuelled endless dreams of faraway lands and unknown creatures, sparking within us a curiosity for worlds beyond our island shores.

Arithmetic was also a big part of our schooling. We committed the twelve times table to memory, and it became a source of both pride and competition. Our teacher would arrange races, challenging us to recite the tables as fast as we could, and we would race to beat each other without making any mistakes. To this day, the twelve times table remains hard-wired in my brain, along with the 'days in the month' rhyme that we often repeated:

"Thirty days hath September, April, June, and November,
All the rest have thirty-one,
Except for February alone,
Which has twenty-eight days each year,
And twenty-nine in a leap year."

Reciting these over and over, competing to see who could do it fastest, is a memory I hold fondly. The rhythm and rhyme of those chants created a bond between us and the lessons we learned, showing me how simple, repetitive acts can etch themselves deeply into one's memory, becoming part of the person you carry into adulthood.

In the final year of primary school, as was the custom across Fiji, we would sit for the Intermediate Entrance Examination. This test would determine if we could continue our education beyond class five. Those who passed would be offered a place in an intermediate school on one of the two largest islands, where we would continue through to class eight. If our pass was good enough we would be offered a scholarship to board in one of these schools. Other students might have relatives near a school with whom they could board. Otherwise, formal education would likely end. We would stay on the island, helping our families with farming and leading a subsistence life. To me and many of my classmates, this exam felt like a key, a chance to unlock a future that seemed just out of reach, a future we could not fully imagine but longed for, nonetheless.

For students in urban areas, this path seemed much more achievable. They were already close to an intermediate school, they were exposed to the English language more, and they had access to more resources. But for those of us living on remote islands like Moala, it felt like a distant dream. The hurdles were immense— transport was difficult, boat fares were expensive and opportunities were few. Yet despite these barriers, the dream of going further kept a small light of hope flickering within us.

I remember vividly the excitement of the move from our church 'school' to our new school building at Vagavi, just outside the village. Suddenly, we were a real primary school with two trained teachers. It was a sense of legitimacy, a small triumph that made us feel our future might hold something beyond the island. The head teacher, Waqa Likusuasua, was a first cousin of mine, and his deputy, Ratu Nacanieli Draunidalo, would soon become my brother-in-law. The school was called Naroi District School and, for many of us, it became a source of pride—this was where it all began for those of us who went on to challenging roles in government or the private sector.

As I mentioned earlier, the school only went up to class five. For those of us lucky enough to continue, the top boys' schools were Ratu Kadavulevu School or Lelean Memorial School. For girls, it was Adi Cakobau School or Ballantyne Memorial School.

Looking back, I feel a sense of nostalgia for those days. I often recall the innocence of our existence, and the long, languid days spent at school. The classroom sat perched on a hill, offering a beautiful view of the clear blue waters of the village bay, stretching out from the white sandy beach to the endless horizon. The sky seemed to go on forever, and when lessons were held outside, under the shade of a large mango tree, the teacher's voice would blend with the sound of the surf and the rustling of leaves in the sea breeze. In those moments, learning felt as natural as breathing, as though the land itself were teaching us. I can still picture those peaceful scenes in my mind as clearly as if they had happened yesterday.

One of the highlights of the school year was the annual drama performance, where we would put on plays to entertain the village. I remember one particular performance that made me realise I had a hidden talent for improvisation. I played a young boy trying to placate an angry girl and, when I forgot my lines, I quickly improvised, offering her my belt as a bribe in exchange for her silence. The audience roared with laughter and, for a brief moment, I felt a spark of confidence that would later serve me well in life. Those moments of spontaneity and resilience, though small, were seeds of the skills that would guide me through the complexities of adulthood.

I often think back to those days when we would share our dreams for the future, standing under that wide, endless sky. We all had our own ideas of what we wanted to become. For me, I wanted to be respected— perhaps a pastor or a teacher, as they were the most respected figures in the village. It was not surprising, given the way I often felt about being a child of mixed heritage, caught between two worlds. But practical considerations weighed heavily on me. My elder brother George had already passed the Intermediate Exam and was attending Lelean Memorial School on the main island. My stepfather did not think it was necessary for both of us boys to be educated, and certainly not my sister. His plan for me was simple: I was to stay in the village and help with the family's food gardens, providing extra labour.

My mother, however, had a different vision. She wanted me to become a church minister—a respected and honourable path in her eyes. I did not mind the thought; in fact, I found it appealing as it was a role that could bring respect and purpose. But with my stepfather set against the idea; any plan to take me away from the village and further my education seemed out of reach.

CHAPTER 5

A SECOND CHANCE

Whatever I wished for, or whatever plans my mother or stepfather had, one thing was certain: I was still at school, and I had to finish my village schooling before anything else could be decided. Little did I know that the path ahead was already shifting, and fate was quietly preparing to intervene on my behalf.

In 1955, I sat for the Intermediate Examination, a pivotal moment for any village child with dreams of a future beyond the island. To my surprise and immense relief, I passed. Not only that, but I was also offered a scholarship to attend Ratu Kadavulevu School (RKS) the following year—an honour that felt like a rare gift. Only one other student from our village had ever achieved this before. But my stepfather, Taoka, ever stern, calculating and unbending, refused to allow it. To him, my education had reached its conclusion. I was to remain in the village to tend to the gardens and work alongside him, a future that felt painfully small, a future of unrealised dreams and narrowing horizons.

But it seemed fate had other plans; plans I could not yet see unfolding in the quiet corners of my life.

At that time, my elder half-sister, Sera, had married Ratu Nacanieli Draunidalo, one of the village teachers. He believed in me and saw a glimmer of academic potential. He argued that, at just ten years old, I should be allowed to stay in school for at least one more year before being condemned to a life of hard labour. Knowing Sera, with her quiet and unyielding resolve behind the scenes, must have firmly pushed for this chance. Together, they secured one more year for me—a reprieve, a brief extension of hope.

In 1956, I sat for the examination again. And, once more, I passed. Once more, a scholarship to RKS was offered. But my stepfather stood firm in his refusal. The opportunity slipped through my fingers yet again. By the beginning of 1957, the new school term had started, and I was no longer attending. Instead, I remained in the village, labouring away in our food garden, feeling as though my fate was already sealed—my dreams of further education were slipping away for good.

But fate had not given up on me just yet.

One morning in late February 1957, a young medical officer from the island of Kadavu, Dr Buru, who had recently been appointed to Moala, was listening to the news on his radio. As was his habit, he tuned in for community announcements. That morning, a broadcast from RKS called for students whose places had been reserved but who had yet to arrive. Among the names listed was mine. Although Dr Buru did not know me personally, he recognised the name of my village and made a note. Later that day, when he attended the village meeting, he brought the announcement to the attention of the elders.

To this day, I do not know what words were spoken in that meeting, only that they were enough to move my stepfather and the elders to action. This opportunity— this chance to learn—could no longer be ignored.

And so, with a sense of urgency, my eldest half-brother, Kata, my cousins Mika and Joeli and I set to work. We needed to collect and cut enough copra to cover the boat fare and purchase the basic supplies required for school—each piece of equipment and clothing a small step towards a future unknown but deeply longed for. I still remember some of the essentials we were asked to bring with us, each item feeling more significant than it might seem to others:

- 2 or 3 white shirts
- 2 or 3 white pocket sulus
- 4 pairs of underpants
- 2 pairs of work shorts
- 1 pair of sports shorts
- 2 white vests
- 1 cane knife and file
- 1 mosquito net
- A traditional wooden spear and club for cultural performances
- A comb, toothbrush, toothpaste, straw mats, a pillow and towels

To me, these were more than mere supplies: they were symbols of a nascent education pilgrimage.

By March, everything was ready. All that remained was waiting for the next boat to Suva—a boat that would carry me into a future I had barely dared to imagine. At just eleven years old, I had never left Moala, and the thought of travelling to Suva filled me with both wonder and anxiety. My stepfather volunteered to accompany me on the boat. The plan was to sell the copra once we reached Suva, use the proceeds to purchase the required items then he was to go with me by bus to RKS—a journey that felt as though it would carry me across worlds. In theory, it seemed all set.

The anticipation in the days leading up to my departure was electric, a strange mix of excitement and trepidation.

Every evening, as I prepared the *yaqona* for the village elders, they began to offer me bits of advice— what to do, what to avoid and the hidden dangers of the 'big smoke.' To them, this was no ordinary journey; it was a once-in-a-lifetime adventure. In those days, a trip to Suva was like travelling overseas—rare, expensive and full of mystery. I listened to their stories, feeling a mixture of excitement and anxiety. They were trying to prepare me for a world beyond anything I had known, an adventure that seemed both thrilling and daunting, as foreign to me as the city of Suva itself.

One evening, the village storyteller, Waqa Avenisi, pulled me aside and gave me a warning I will never forget. He told me to watch out for the *motoka*—the automobiles. "They're like big pigs with glaring eyes," he said. At that point, I had never seen a motorised vehicle, not even a bicycle. I knew a *motoka* was some kind of transport, but in my mind I pictured a giant pig with people inside its belly. The image, vivid and absurd, both amused and unnerved me, feeding my already active imagination and adding to the curious patchwork of stories I carried with me.

"This is indeed a trip of a lifetime," I thought to myself, a mixture of awe and apprehension swirling within me and a strange sense that my life was about to change.

As the weeks passed and the boat's arrival drew nearer, I found myself in a constant state of suspended animation, unable to think of anything else. The adventure ahead felt like a dream, hovering just beyond my grasp. Every moment, I held my breath, waiting for fate to carry me across the waters to a future I could hardly envision—one that felt distant and unreal, yet tantalisingly close.

Chapter 6

An introduction to Suva—a city of lights and dreams

Finally, the boat, the M.V. Melenisia, arrived, and my stepfather and I boarded it in the mid-afternoon. I remember the farewells—my mother and sisters in tears while waving us off. The M.V. Melenisia was an inter-island copra carrier, just about 10 metres long, with a single diesel engine and backup sails. I had only ever been in coastal traditional canoes and dinghies before. This was my first-ever boat trip beyond the reef, and I was full of excitement, mingled with a nervous energy I could not quite contain.

But excitement quickly gave way to fear. March, after all, was still hurricane season in Fiji, and we had the misfortune of hitting severe weather. The small boat was tossed about like a cork in the raging sea. Between bouts of seasickness and moments of sheer terror, I found myself wishing I could be back in Moala, where everything was simple and safe. In those dark hours, as the waves rose higher and the boat pitched beneath us, I clung to my seat, silently vowing never to leave my island again. But we made it through the storm, and by dawn the next day, after 14 exhausting hours, we reached Suva.

I will never forget my first glimpse of the city. Far out at sea, as the boat approached, I saw the lights of Suva twinkling on the horizon, and my heart raced with excitement. I was awestruck. How could lights be so bright that they reached us all the way out here? The soft glow seemed otherworldly. I had never seen electricity before and, in my young mind, I believed these must be powerful benzene or kerosene lamps which were used in the village. I admired their strength and wondered, "If only we could have such lights in our village, *cina lairo* (hunting land crabs in the dark using kerosene lamps) would be so much easier."

As we drew closer, I could see that these lights were attached to tall poles, perfectly aligned along the shore, their glow steady and strong. They were far brighter than the kerosene lamps I was familiar with, so I reasoned they must be enormous benzene lamps which were brighter. My imagination ran wild, trying to picture how anyone could climb these poles each night to light them. I even tried to imagine the teams of men who would have to keep these lamps burning, climbing the poles, pumping the lamps every hour to keep them lit and bright. "Hundreds of men must work all night to keep the lights of Suva shining!" I thought to myself. It was a city of marvels and magic.

My fascination deepened as I spotted lights in pairs, moving quickly along the roads. These had to be the "pigs with glaring eyes" that Waqa Avenisi had warned me about. They moved at an unimaginable speed, and I could not quite comprehend how they glided along the streets. My young mind tried to keep up with the flood of new sensations, the overwhelming mix of awe and confusion that hit me all at once. Everything I had ever known seemed so insignificant compared to this city of light and speed. Even the air seemed alive, buzzing with a hum that echoed the city's energy. I stood by the ship's railing, silent, taking it all in, my mind whirling with wonder and a bit of fear.

As we drew closer to the dock, I saw more clearly the shapes of these moving "pigs." The sounds of the engines and the occasional blasts of their horns—like deep oinks—added to the chaos of the moment. I watched in awe as the world of Suva began to unfold before me. The wharf was alive with activity, the city coming to life before my eyes. People moved with purpose, trucks and cars zipped by, and the world seemed to move at a pace I could barely comprehend.

It was all too much for me. My young mind could only take in so much before everything blurred into a dizzying whirl of colours and sounds, like a windvane spinning so fast that its individual blades merged into a single white blur. I stood frozen, overwhelmed by the sheer enormity of this new world. The city felt alive, breathing and pulsating with its own rhythm—a stark contrast to the quite steadiness of Moala. I felt then that I had seen things I never imagined possible.

If only I had known then that this was just the beginning of an adventure that would take me far beyond Suva. If only I had known then that one day I would find myself travelling the world, climbing the ranks of a multinational company, leading men and women to build even more complex machines than the ones before me. If only I had known then that I would one day look these 'minor gods' in the eye as an equal. And if only I had known then that I would marry not one but two women of this 'minor god' race—one wild and passionate, the other my spiritual companion, my best friend, my deep love. But all that was still to come, for now, I was lost in dizzy bewilderment.

My attention was drawn back to the towering buildings of Suva. The tallest building was only three storeys high but, to a village boy, it seemed to scrape the sky. My frame of reference for 'tall' was the height of a coconut tree, yet these buildings rose higher than any coconut tree I had ever seen. I watched, wide-eyed, as the city stirred to life. The fresh morning air was clean from the night's rain, and the streets bustled with activity. I could see the market near the wharf coming to life, vendors setting up their stalls, and the chaotic sounds of produce being unloaded and arranged. The rhythmic calls of peanut vendors rang out—"bean-peanut, bean-peanut"—mingling with the revving of engines from the buses at the nearby station.

The buses themselves were a source of wonder—moving mountains of steel and sound. They were massive machines, much larger than anything I had imagined, and they seemed to swallow up people as they clambered aboard. Their dirty exhaust smoke began to fill the morning air, mixing with the fresh rain smell and reminding me that this was a place of movement and speed, a place where life moved faster than I had ever known.

"Ba!" (my village nickname, short for Banivanua), I heard my stepfather call out, breaking me from my trance. He was waving me over to join him in an open-air carrier where our belongings were already loaded. I was about to ride in one of these machines at last! It was not a bus or car with a 'stomach' as I had imagined, but it was thrilling all the same. I climbed into the back, clutching the sides for dear life as the carrier sped through the streets of Suva. The rush of air and the blur of sights were exhilarating and, for a moment, fear and excitement collided as the city whizzed past me. The ride was short, but the impact was lasting—the city had left its mark on me.

And thus began my introduction to Suva—a world of wonders, a city of light and dreams.

CHAPTER 7

LOST IN THE CITY AND THE COPPER GANG

My stepfather delivered me to a relative's place in Turaki, a suburb of Suva, then disappeared with a vague promise that he would return to take me to RKS. He did not say when, and neither did he inform my hosts. I was left waiting, trusting he would come back soon. Days passed, but Taoka never returned.

My hosts were distant relatives: Mele, who came from Moala like me, and her husband Bose, a man from Rewa on the main island. They lived in a cramped one-room servant's quarters with their three sons—Siti, Esala and Tui. The boys ran wild, rarely attending school, and life seemed a constant struggle for the family. Mele and Bose were too busy trying to scrape together a living to worry much about where their boys wandered, and now I had become another mouth to feed.

Taoka's absence stretched on. A day turned into a week, then weeks. In my eleven-year-old innocence, I still believed he would return to take me to RKS. But time wore on, and I was left in limbo, my hope fading slowly as each day passed. I later learned that Taoka had disappeared somewhere else with the money from the sale of our copra. The money that Kata, Mika, Joeli and I had worked so hard to gather was gone and, with it, my immediate hope of getting to school. Taoka and the money were nowhere to be seen.

In the meantime, I followed Siti everywhere, as though this new way of life was simply part of the adventure. We roamed the streets, and one day he introduced me to a peculiar new activity: collecting empty milk bottles. We found bottles in front of houses and took them to a nearby Chinese-run milk bar to sell. I had no idea at the time that people left these bottles out for the milkman to exchange for fresh milk. To me, it seemed like a natural thing to do—picking up bottles, selling them and using the money to buy treats felt like an innocent hustle, a simple part of our city lives.

It was through this 'bottle collecting' that I had my first taste of ice cream and milkshakes. To a boy from Moala, these were flavours that felt like pure magic, far better than our village *lolis*. I still remember the first icy sweetness of ice cream melting on my tongue—rich and impossibly cold. The moment that cold sweetness hit my tongue, I was hooked, and it was not long before Siti introduced me to his larger group of friends. These boys called themselves the copper gang.

Our day started at early dawn, spent in this newfound 'bottle collection' routine, but by day we had another focus—trawling the Nabukalou Creek. The goal was simple: find any scrap metal, especially copper, to sell to a scrap metal dealer. It was a new game, and one that brought quick money. Before long, our nightly adventures escalated. We built a makeshift tin boat—a *bavelo*—and would row silently under the cover of darkness towards the Post & Telegraph depot in Walu Bay. With great stealth, we would pull strips of copper cables through the fence and sell them off the next day to Bish Ltd, an engineering shop cum scrap metal dealer.

At eleven, I was too young to fully grasp the consequences of what we were doing. In the village, when you were hungry, you could go to the bush and pick fruit or dig up wild yams. But Suva was different. Hunger here meant you hunted for copper or bottles—anything that could be sold for a quick meal, whether it was an ice cream, a meat pie or a drink. It was so easy to fall into this life of petty thievery, and I did. It felt thrilling to belong, to be part of something, and these boys—Fijians, Indians, and mixed-race kids—never teased me about being half Chinese. We all fit together in this strange, bustling city.

They also introduced me to the world of cinema. Movie theatres became a new addiction. I had never experienced anything like the flashing images on a screen, the sounds and stories that seemed to transport me to another world. Along with the ice cream, milkshakes and meat pies, cinema became part of my new addiction. It felt like pure magic—far removed from the quiet simplicity of my village.

But it was this newfound love for cinema that led to one of the most terrifying moments of my life—a rude awakening that would save me from a path that, sadly, many of my newfound friends would follow. Most of the boys in the gang, including Siti, would eventually be taken to the 'Borstal School,' the reformatory for young criminals in Suva. Some would later end up in prison. The Borstal School, in my view, did more harm than good, leaving those boys marked and outcast, feeding the very criminal careers it sought to prevent. I was fortunate enough to avoid this fate.

The turning point came with my obsession with a hypnotist who came to Suva to perform at the Phoenix Theatre, one of the four cinemas in town. Siti and I were determined to see the hypnotist on stage and to experience the magic of the show. But, of course, we had no money for tickets. So, we hatched a plan. We snuck into the theatre's garden, hiding in the bushes and peeking through the side doors to watch. We were completely captivated, lost in the magic of the hypnotist's performance, but we got careless. A staff member spotted us.

Suddenly, midway through the show, I felt a strong hand grab my collar. The police had been called, and Siti and I were dragged into the manager's office. My heart pounded with fear, my mind racing with the consequences of what we had done. I was sure we were going to be arrested. Luckily, the theatre owner, a *palagi*, saw something in us—perhaps a young boy's innocent fascination—and chose not to press charges. The police let us off with a stern lecture.

That scare was enough for me. From that day on, I vowed to stop these risky exploits. Even if it meant going hungry, I would collect only beer bottles, scavenge for genuine scrap metal and stick to playing marbles on the street. It was mid-April by then, six weeks since I had arrived, and the school term had long begun. Taoka was still nowhere in sight. Eventually, I learned much later, he did return to the village, where he remained for years to come. What he told my mother upon his return, I could only imagine, but knowing him, it was unlikely to be the truth.

Meanwhile, I roamed the streets of Suva with Siti and his friends. Then, one day, in the middle of a marble game, I felt a hand on my shoulder. It was my cousin,

Apenisa Ravula, who recognised me on the street. He looked at me with concern and asked why I was not at school. I told him the story—how I had been waiting for Taoka, how the days had turned into weeks and how I did not know what to do. Apenisa must have realised that my wait would be in vain. Without hesitation, he took me in.

Though Apenisa's family lived in a cramped, single rented room, it was a welcome change. Now, I had a roof over my head, a decent meal and the comfort of being with closer family. Apenisa, or Roko Ave as we called him, worked as a night watchman and, even though his wages were meagre, he scraped together enough to buy my school supplies and bus fare. Through his quiet generosity, he rekindled a hope I thought was lost. Two weeks later, I was finally on my way to Lodoni, the site of RKS.

CHAPTER 8

LODONI AND A JOURNEY
OF FEAR AND HOPE

After two weeks with Roko Ave's family, it was time for the next chapter of my adventure. We said our goodbyes and, with a mix of excitement and gratitude, I followed him as we carried my boarding school luggage down to the central bus station. This was my first-ever long bus trip and, although I was eager to experience something new, my heart was heavy with appreciation for Roko Ave, who had made sacrifices to get me this far.

The bus to Lodoni ran twice a day—once in the morning and once in the afternoon. We caught the afternoon bus, which meant we would arrive just before dusk. The trip was about an hour and a half long, but the road was rough, unsealed and full of bumps. By the time we reached Lodoni, we were covered head to toe in red dust. I had heard the stories: passengers arriving unrecognisable, with hair and clothes tinted 'ginger' from the dust cloud kicked up by the bus. It felt like a rite of passage, a humorous initiation into a new chapter of life.

But dust turned out to be the least of my problems. I had never experienced such a long journey in the 'belly' of a bus before, and the combination of the rough road and the diesel fumes made me terribly carsick. The excitement of the trip quickly faded as my stomach churned with every twist and turn. I felt embarrassed and miserable but, luckily, the bus had no windows as such, just open sides with tarpaulins to let down in case of rain. Some wit had called it 'free air conditioning.' At least I could lean out to be sick without bothering too many passengers. Every corner seemed like it would be the end of me. By the time we finally reached our destination, I was more than ready to get off the bus.

As soon as we arrived, my eyes were drawn to something I had never seen before: cane toads. The ground, still wet from the previous day's rain, was covered with them—hundreds of these strange, prehistoric-looking creatures hopping around in every direction. I had never encountered toads in Moala, and I had not seen any in Suva either, so these creatures were as foreign to me as the city itself. I froze in fear as they leapt towards me, seemingly unafraid of humans and with a look that made me feel as if they had some hostile intent. I let out a shriek, convinced they were coming for me. It was only when Roko Ave explained that they were harmless toads that I calmed down a little. Still, they gave me nightmares for weeks. Even after that day, I could never quite shake the feeling that they were watching me, waiting for the right moment to hop my way.

Our arrival must have caused some curiosity among the students, as it was unusual to see someone arrive so late into the term. Years later, a friend who had been at the school at the time told me he remembered the day I arrived. He said I looked every bit the "village boy"— or, as he put it, "primitive and unsophisticated"—wide-eyed, barefoot and clutching a wooden suitcase. Everything I had with me spoke of my simple village life.

My suitcase was a massive wooden case, likely brought over by my father from China, its camphor skin peeling with age. It was so large that, back in the village, I used to hide inside it when we played hide-and-seek. In fact, two of me could have fitted comfortably inside with room to spare. My *wau* (club) for dances was an authentic war club from my grandfather, so heavy that I could barely lift it, let alone use it for dancing! My coconut oil bottles were carried in a traditional *noke*—a woven basket that had long gone out of style in the city. To top it off, I spoke the Moala dialect, which no one there understood. I must have been a strange and amusing sight to my peers, like a lost animal, caught in the headlights of a strange and fast-moving world.

But luckily, there was a teacher at RKS from Moala—Cava Buadromo. With some help from Roko Ave, we found Cava, who took charge of my arrival. He helped sort out my dormitory assignment—Building 17—and my house, which was Sukuna House. I was placed in class 6A. With that, my transition to RKS was complete.

The next day, I said farewell to Roko Ave as he boarded the bus back to Suva. As I watched the bus disappear around the bend, a deep wave of loneliness washed over me. The full weight of my journey, of all the strangeness and unfamiliarity, hit me like a crashing wave. I was just eleven years old, in a place that felt a world away from home, surrounded by people I did not know who spoke a dialect I barely understood. For the first time, I felt truly alone. My entire world seemed to crumble around me and, before I could stop myself, I broke down in tears. I sobbed, not knowing who or what I was crying for—just that I had never felt so small, so far from home, and so afraid.

On top of it all, I feared being teased again for being *kai jaina* in this Fijian boys' boarding school. Would I be bullied? Who would stand up for me here? There were no relatives to protect me, no familiar faces to give me strength. I was probably the smallest boy (measuring just three feet, ten inches on arrival) in the whole school, and I had no idea how I could fight back if it came to that. If I could have turned around and gone back to the village right then and there, I would have done it in a heartbeat. The safety and simplicity of Moala beckoned.

But there was no turning back.

When the tears finally stopped, I sat down and tried to make sense of it all. I had come so far, faced so many hurdles, and here I was—finally at RKS. Maybe I was overwhelmed, but I was not broken. I asked myself, "What's the worst that could happen?" I would miss my mother and my friends, yes, but I would see them again. The first term was almost over, and I knew it would be hard to make friends. I would probably get teased, and I might even get into a fight and come out the loser. But what were a few black eyes compared to the chance of getting an education? The thought of returning to Moala, of giving up this once-in-a-lifetime opportunity, filled me with regret as I weighed my fears against my dreams.

So, I made up my mind. I would face whatever came my way. Armed with this small sense of determination, I stood up, wiped my eyes, and walked back to my dormitory to face this strange new world—and the 300 boys who lived in it.

CHAPTER 9

FORGED IN DISCIPLINE—LIFE AND LOYALTY AT RKS

Dormitory number 17 was a long, narrow wooden hut, much like the others at RKS, where I found myself stepping into a new chapter of life. There were eight identical dormitories when I arrived, with two more to be added later. Each pair of dormitories made up a house, and there were four houses in total: Sukuna, Ma'afu, Degei and Cakau. I was assigned to Sukuna House, where the boys of Dormitories 17 and 18 were brought together.

Walking into the hut for the first time, I was struck by its length and narrowness. To the eyes of an eleven-year-old, the dormitory felt enormous, stretching endlessly with its repetitive rows of wooden beds along either side with a narrow corridor running between them. The sunlight filtered through the windows, yet the confined space felt overwhelming. The beds were simple with no mattresses—just bare boards on which we spread our straw mats. For the first time in my life, I was sleeping on a bed instead of the floor, a novelty but a strange and exciting change, nevertheless.

Each hut housed around forty boys, and the thought of so many of us sleeping side by side was both intimidating and exhilarating. There was a sense of camaraderie in knowing we were all in this together. My bed was next to a boy named Isimeli Bose from the Yasawa Islands. Like me, he had come straight from his village, and there was something reassuring in having someone just as new to this experience by my side. Little did I know that this bond would grow into a lifelong friendship; he would later become a government minister, but back then, we were just two boys trying to navigate an unfamiliar world.

Life at RKS was a regimented dance of discipline and routine. It was not long before we started to joke that the school felt like living in a detention camp. In some ways, it truly did. Every morning at six sharp, the deep, resonant sound of the *lali*—a hollowed-out wooden drum—would echo across the campus, commanding us to rise. Bleary-eyed and barely awake, I would fumble into my work clothes, grab my cane knife, and join the others for our morning duties. Some boys were 'house boys,' allocated to each teacher household and responsible for chopping firewood, starting stoves and tending the teacher's gardens. For the rest of us, mornings were filled with clearing the school grounds, cutting grass or weeding with our cane knives.

Hard physical labour was not foreign to me. Growing up in the village had prepared me well; my hands were already accustomed to the rhythms of swinging a cane knife, tending to food gardens and performing daily chores. Throwing myself into this work was also a way to manage the homesickness that gnawed at me during those first few weeks. The steady rhythm of the blade cutting through grass became a comforting distraction, each swing dulling the ache of being away from home.

At seven o'clock, the *lali* would sound again, signalling that it was time to head back to the dormitory. We would wash up, dress quickly and head to breakfast, all the while keeping an eye on the clock. Afterwards, each boy would make his bed, tidying his space in preparation for the dreaded inspection. Failing inspection often meant additional chores, so we made sure everything was in order. There was no room for slackness.

Classes began at nine and went on until 3:30 p.m., after which we were greeted by more laborious tasks—cutting more grass, chopping firewood or tending to the school food gardens. Finally, after all the work, we would be allowed an hour of free time before dinner. That precious hour was often spent playing sports, chatting with friends or hurriedly doing our laundry. Prep time was after dinner to 8.30 pm, and 9 p.m. was lights-out. The days were long, structured and physically demanding, leaving little room for rest.

Saturdays were split between hard labour in the mornings and free time in the afternoons—unless, of course, you were being punished. In such cases, the luxury of relaxing afternoons was stripped away leaving only the monotony of endless chores. For the rest of us, afternoons were a chance to escape into the bush. I naturally gravitated towards activities like prawning in the streams nearby or digging for wild yams. These little excursions brought back a taste of the village life I missed, and I relished them as a way to supplement our often-meagre meals.

Sundays, in contrast, were days cloaked in the quiet, secure rhythm of Christian Sunday holiness, offering a reprieve from the grind. The familiar call of the *lali* signalled church services throughout the day. The hymns, prayers and structure of Sunday worship felt like an anchor, grounding me in a world that often felt chaotic and far from home. For one day, the harsh edges of discipline softened, and we found comfort in the rituals that felt like a reminder of who we were and where we came from.

The meals at RKS were simple but filling, though they paled in comparison to the fresh feasts of village life. Cassava and tea, often *draunimoli* tea, were staples of breakfast. Occasionally, we were served plain rice and, on rare days, we were treated to home-baked bread— though it was more like half-baked dough, dense and almost impossible to chew. Still, we cherished it as a rare treat. I look back now and marvel at how something so basic could become the highlight of the month.

Lunch was a monotonous rotation of boiled vegetables like *bele* or Chinese cabbage, served with more cassava. If we were lucky, there would be a hint of tinned fish, though finding an actual piece was a rare blessing. Dinner was more of the same, though some nights we had a stew made of bones and tough meat. Despite its sparsity, the stew was always welcomed.

Sports were the lifeblood of RKS. Rugby and athletics were at the heart of our school identity, and our fiercest rivalry was with Queen Victoria School (QVS), just fifteen kilometres down the road. The rivalry extended beyond the field; it was about honour, loyalty and earning a year's worth of bragging rights. A victory over QVS was more than just a win—it was a badge of esteem that could influence everything from introductions to the girls at Adi Cakobau School to job prospects later in life.

Though I was too small for contact sports, I found my place in the cheer squad. As a cheerleader, I poured my heart into every match, feeling each victory and defeat as deeply as if I were on the field. One loss in particular still stings—a defeat decided by a last-minute penalty kick. For a week, the entire school mourned, teachers included. I lost my voice from the shouting, but the sense of camaraderie and shared sorrow was unforgettable.

Ultimately, RKS was about forging boys into men, preparing us for practical, technical careers, while QVS was the gateway to academic qualifications and future leadership. At the end of my three years in the intermediate section, I sat for the Secondary Schools Entrance Examination. To my surprise, I passed with flying colours, opening the door to transfer to QVS. But my loyalty to RKS had grown deep, and I was torn. I could not help but feel a sense of betrayal at the thought of leaving.

It took the persuasion of my principal Mr. Donnelly and my relative Cava Buadromo to convince me that this was an opportunity not to be missed. Reluctantly, I agreed, though my heart remained heavy.

Looking back, it was a pivotal decision that would change the course of my life. Had I stayed out of loyalty to RKS, who knows how different my journey might have been? But I had learned that, sometimes, loyalty means recognising the chance to grow—even if it means letting go of the familiar.

CHAPTER 10

THE BUDDING ENGINEER—A SPARK OF CURIOSITY AND A JOURNEY OF COURAGE

The school's electricity generator was used sparingly, and each dormitory had designated days for ironing. It was in the small ironing shed on one of those allocated days that the seed of my ambition to become an electrical engineer was first planted.

Every Wednesday was Dormitory 17's turn to use the ironing room. I had not brought an iron with me, naturally assuming they would be provided—just like back in the village, where we used charcoal irons. Ironing at home was almost ceremonial: collecting dried coconut shells, burning them to create charcoal and heating the iron over the glowing embers. I naively expected the same process at RKS. But when no one mentioned it, I kept quiet, unwilling to reveal my ignorance. Instead, I chose to observe.

When Wednesday arrived, we were paraded, as was the routine, from the dormitory to the ironing room. The moment we entered, the older boys rushed forward, snatching up irons and heading straight to the benches. I watched, fascinated. These irons looked somewhat familiar, but there was one significant difference—a cord was attached to each one. The boys quickly plugged these cords into the wall and, to my amazement, a tiny red light appeared above each socket.

I stood in silent awe, my mind racing.

"The heat must be coming from that red light," I thought to myself, feeling a surge of pride at my deduction. But how could it be? There was no fire, no smoke, yet the boys were pressing their clothes, and the creases disappeared just as if they were using a charcoal iron. Determined to uncover the mystery, I decided to wait until the room was empty.

Half an hour later, when the room had cleared, I approached one of the irons with cautious curiosity. I gingerly touched it and found it was still warm. I felt along the cord that connected it to the wall, but it was cool to the touch. This puzzled me—how could heat travel through something cold? My fingers traced up to the red bulb, which was also warm to the touch.

"Aha! So, it is the bulb that's generating the heat," I thought triumphantly. But how? I was determined to get to the bottom of it.

My curiosity got the better of me. I unscrewed the red bulb, convinced I would find something inside—perhaps charcoal hidden within. But when I peered into the socket and poked my finger inside—*ZAP!*

"Ouch!" I yelled as a sharp jolt of electricity shot through me, sending me sprawling to the floor. My whole body tingled, and I sat there, stunned, nursing a small burn on my finger. That day, I learned my first painful lesson about electricity. Never again would I stick my fingers into unknown sockets, but that jolt of curiosity had awakened something in me. I could not shake the desire to understand how this strange force worked. How could it create heat without fire? What had just zapped me?

That shocking moment, painful as it was, felt like an initiation into a world of mystery and discovery. I simply had to know.

Eight years later, during my interview for an Australian Commonwealth Scholarship to study electrical engineering, I would recount this very story when asked why I wanted to pursue this field. The incident that had shocked me—quite literally—had sparked a lifelong passion, one that I am convinced won me the scholarship.

~~~

The school year was divided into three terms punctuated by short breaks and a long Christmas vacation. During my three years at RKS, I never once went to see my family. For some boys like me from the outlying islands, holidays were spent in quite isolation far from home, either because there were no funds for travel or no close relatives in the main island of Viti Levu. In my case there were certainly no funds, but I also felt bad imposing myself on to close relatives, such as Roko Ave's, when they had so little. Instead, I found odd bob-a-jobs working for teachers to save up enough money for a planned boat trip to Moala to see my mother sometime in the future. Did I miss my family? Of course. But, after a while, you become institutionalised. I convinced myself I was here for them—that this opportunity was a gift, one I could not waste.

Yet not everyone managed the separation as well. I remember Semiti Koroi, a fellow Moalan, who would run away the day after his father dropped him off each holiday. His homesickness was too much to bear. To cheer him up, I broke a few school rules with him and another boy, Lasarusa Waqa. On Sundays, after lunch, we would sneak away, walking the fifteen miles to the nearest small town, Korovou, skipping Sunday school to buy ice blocks and sweets. We would catch the bus back, feeling invincible—until the day we found Master Rupeni sitting in the bus. He did not say a word but, come Monday morning, we each received three lashes from his infamous *qanuya* cane. That ended our little adventures.

In the 1958 long Christmas vacation, driven by a spirit of adventure, I decided to set out on my own to visit my elder brother, Jone, whom I had never met. He lived in the bustling goldmining town of Vatukoula, about 200 miles away from school, which in those days might just as well be a thousand miles away. I had never been there, nor had any idea what Jone looked like, nor did I have an address, except for Vatukoula. But I trusted in the village system—someone would surely guide me.

I began planning my journey. I would use some of my hard-earned 'bob-a-job' savings for bus fares, first to Suva then to Vatukoula. I also had to figure out where I could sleep in Suva. I remembered the large copra sheds near the Suva waterfront from when I first arrived. These places were bustling with activity, full of schooners and dockworkers. A small boy sleeping there would not draw any attention. As for food, I knew I could survive on the cheap fruits—bananas and pawpaws—sold at the nearby market.

I packed my belongings into a battered suitcase, rolled up my straw mat and caught the bus from school to Suva. Everything went as planned. I found a quiet corner in the copra shed, settled in for the night and rose early to catch the Sunbeam bus to Vatukoula. The journey was long and rough, the road a dusty red ribbon that stretched on endlessly. By the time I arrived, I was exhausted and covered in dust.

Stepping off the bus in Matanagata, one of Vatukoula's settlements, I was faced with the reality that I had no idea where to go. I approached a shopkeeper, asking if he knew Jone. He did not, but kindly allowed me to wait while he asked his customers. Dusk fell, and just as I began to worry, a young man approached.

"Are you Ba?" he asked.

"Yes," I replied, nervously hopeful. "Are you Jone?"

It was him—my elder brother who had left Moala before I was born. Though he could not accommodate me himself, he found a Moalan couple who graciously took me in for the holidays. My adventure had succeeded. I had journeyed hundreds of miles on my own, driven by the hope of meeting a brother I had only heard about.

~~~

The years at RKS had passed in a blur of discipline, hard work and small acts of rebellion. There were days of exhaustion and isolation, where homesickness left me feeling hollow and out of place. But there were also moments of small triumphs

As I have already mentioned, by the end of 1959 I had earned a place at QVS, where a new chapter awaited me. But I had also saved enough money not only to take that bus trip to locate Jone, but also to finally take a long-awaited trip back to Moala to see my mother and the rest of the family. I said goodbye to Lodoni and RKS and sailed to Moala.

It had been three long years since I had seen my family, and the homecoming was overwhelming. The news of my acceptance into the prestigious QVS spread quickly. My achievement was no longer seen as mine alone; it had become a shared triumph, a source of pride of the entire village. For them and my family, my success carried profound significance. I was not just a son returning home but a symbol of what was possible, a reflection of their shared hopes and dreams, casting light on what could be achieved with effort and determination. In their eyes, I had brought honour to our small corner of the world.

Yet, this admiration came with its own challenges. Conversations in the village often turned to reverent mentions of my name, something that left me feeling awkward and self-conscious. I was proud to have earned their respect, but the weight of their praise sometimes felt heavy. It was humbling to be elevated in this way, yet unsettling to be treated as though I had already reached some lofty pinnacle. I considered my accomplishments as mere steps in a much larger journey. Still, I learned to see the value in their pride. If my story could inspire others—if it could plant seeds of ambition in the next generation—then the discomfort was a small price to pay. I saw myself then as part of a ripple effect that might uplift those around me.

In January 1960, the time came for me to leave once more—this time to begin my journey to QVS. As the ship pulled away from Moala and the island receded into the soft glow of the sunset, I stood at the rail, the salty breeze carrying a mix of emotions. There was a twinge of sadness in that moment, though I did not realise it would be twenty-six years before I would walk its shores once more. This farewell was more than just a goodbye; it marked the end of one chapter and the beginning of another—a chapter of broader horizons and even greater challenges.

The ship docked in Suva early the next morning. As I boarded the bus that would take me north, I felt a mixture of anticipation and resolve. I was leaving behind the familiarity of Lodoni and routines of RKS, venturing further to Matavatucou to begin the next step at QVS. It was a journey into the unknown, but I carried with me the hopes of my family and the pride of my village, each step a testament to the courage and determination that had brought me this far. And, just as I had at RKS, I was ready to embrace the next adventure that lay ahead.

Chapter 11

Queen Victoria School—a new world of expectations

Arriving at QVS, I could already sense that this was a place of higher expectations—a step up from the simpler days at RKS. The list of required items for the school year felt like a preview of the changes to come. Gone were the days of running barefoot and shirtless; for the first time, I was to wear a proper school uniform, complete with sandals. As I looked at myself in the mirror, clad in this new uniform, I realised how far I had come. The transformation from the boy who had once lived in the village and wore little more than a *laplap sulu* was now in full motion. It felt strange, almost like I was stepping into someone else's life.

To get our uniforms made, we had to visit one of the many Indian tailors in Suva, who worked swiftly with their tape measures and sewing machines. Standing still as the tailor's scissors sliced through the fabric, I felt as though my life, too, was being shaped for something new. It felt odd, standing still as they fussed over my measurements, adjusting and cutting fabric as though preparing me for something grander. And maybe, in a way, they were. As I watched the fabric take shape, I felt a strange mix of pride and unease, as if the mere fact of shaping the fabric was symptomatic of the shape of things to come.

QVS itself was a stunning sight, nestled on 205 acres of land in Matavatucou on the main island of Viti Levu. The buildings stood like monuments to learning, carefully arranged amidst the rolling hills. Even though I had left the village far behind, there was something about the natural beauty of the school that made me feel at ease. The layout of the school seemed almost ceremonial, as if every detail—every building and every field—was planned with purpose, reflecting the gravity of what this place represented. The buildings were perched on gentle slopes overlooking the ocean, with two small islands—Qoma Levu and Qoma Lailai—framing the horizon, like quiet sentinels keeping watch over us. Below, a flat expanse of land sprawled out, housing two rugby fields, a running track and a cricket and hockey field. It was like stepping into a postcard, so beautiful and serene, it did not seem real.

The school had been established by the Great Council of Chiefs, modelled after the prestigious public schools of the United Kingdom. Fiji, after all, was still a British colony, and much of the school's tradition was rooted in that legacy. It had been built to educate the sons of chiefs and the brightest boys from all over Fiji, those who were destined to become the future administrators and leaders of the country. The gravity of the place was tangible, the air thick with purpose and expectation. The history of the place weighed heavily in the air, yet there was something exhilarating about walking onto these grounds, knowing that so many before me had passed through these gates on their way to greatness. And though I did not know it at the time, this would be the beginning of my own path into a future I could hardly have imagined.

At the time, QVS was a boarding school for about 400 boys, housed in eight concrete dormitories. The dormitories were sturdier than those at RKS, and there was a marked upgrade in living conditions. Each house was made up of two dormitories, with names steeped in Fijian history: Bau, Rewa, Verata and Tovata. I found myself in Verata House, my new home for the next few years. I was both nervous and excited, imagining what this new 'home' would be like and what lay ahead. The dormitories were much brighter, with large windows allowing natural light to flood the rooms. The beds were metal framed, with springs instead of wooden planks—though mattresses were still not provided, so we laid our straw mats over the springs as we had always done.

For the first time, we were given a chest of drawers for our belongings—a small luxury that felt like a significant leap from the simple lifestyle of my previous schools. It was a subtle but unmistakeable signal that we were stepping into a new world, where order and discipline were paramount, and our education was about more than just learning facts—it was about preparing us for something bigger.

QVS focused exclusively on secondary education, unlike RKS, which also had an intermediate school. Here, boys ranged from 14-year-olds in Form 3 to 19-year-olds in the final year, Form 6. The competition was fierce. Each year, external examinations filtered out those who could not keep up, determining who would advance from Form 4 to Form Lower 5 by passing the Fiji Junior School Certificate examination, and from Form Upper 5 to Form 6 by passing the Cambridge

Senior School Certificate. At the end of Form 6, we sat for the New Zealand University Entrance Examination, which was the key to securing one of the coveted scholarships to study in universities in Australia, New Zealand or even the UK. To get a scholarship, we had to spend another year at Suva Grammar School in the capital, a year known as the Higher Education Course (HEC) year.

Of any given intake of sixty boys, fewer than twenty would survive the academic cull to make it to the final year, and even fewer would go on to university. The stakes were high and, though it felt intimidating, there was also a thrill in knowing that we were part of a system designed to push us to our limits. I felt both excitement and dread at the thought of what lay ahead—each step towards success here meant one step closer to a future I could not quite picture but knew was important

The meals were better than we had at RKS—proper bread and meat twice a week. It felt like a luxury after the meagre rations we were used to. Physical labour was also less intense; we did not have to maintain vegetable gardens or food crops like at RKS. The school grounds were well-kept, with vast lawns, and though we still had to pitch in for maintenance, a tractor-driven mower handled most of the hard work. It almost felt like a holiday resort compared to the ruggedness of my previous school.

The teaching staff was different too. Most of our teachers were *palagis* from Australia, New Zealand, and the UK. Their presence added a new dimension, a clear focus on academic training that felt a world apart from what I had known. The focus seemed clear, education was the primary business. But, despite the academic rigour, QVS still excelled in sports. Our facilities were second to none, and we dominated in rugby and athletics, carrying on the proud traditions of the school's sporting history.

So, it was into this new, enlightened environment that I arrived in 1960, one of sixty new students eager to make our mark. We were awed by the place—the traditions, the history, the structure. Yet beneath it all was a common thread: the boys around me, each eager to prove himself, ambitions buzzing, jostling and laughing but each of us sensing the gravity of our journey here. But make no mistake, as serious as the new regimen seemed, there was still room for mischief. Boys will always be boys, and QVS, with all its grandeur and prestige, was no exception.

There was a shift, though. I could feel it in the air, in the expectations of our teachers and in the quiet understanding among the boys. This was a place where futures were forged. For the first time, I began to truly grasp the importance of the opportunity that lay before me.

CHAPTER 12

MINDS AND TRADITIONS MOULDED

Apart from the lighter load of menial work, daily life at Queen Victoria School was not so different from RKS—but academically, it was like night and day. At RKS, we had been grounded in basics like arithmetic, English, history and Fijian. Now, those familiar subjects gave way to a dizzying array of new disciplines—physics, chemistry, biology, algebra, geometry, geography, English literature and more.

It was a world of knowledge I had never glimpsed before, and it filled me with equal parts excitement and apprehension. "What are all these subjects? And why so many?" These were the questions on the minds of the sixty or so new students, me included, as we stared wide-eyed at our timetables on the first academic day. My heart raced as I looked at the pages, each line brimming with unknown terms—like stepping onto the shore of an unfamiliar land.

Surprisingly, I found myself enjoying the rigours of this new academic regime. It was as though I had stepped into a library of worlds, each subject opening doors to realms of possibilities. In ancient history, I was transported to Egypt, walking alongside the pharaohs. I could imagine the dry heat, the towering pyramids, the ancient streets, and felt the weight of the past through each lesson. I empathised with the early Egyptians, who, much like we had in the village, made do with whatever was available—using papyrus as we had used cowrie shells to 'write' on the church floor in the village. I marvelled at the tale of the Trojan Horse and found myself lost in the legend of the Hanging Gardens of Babylon. These far-off worlds, once unimaginable, now felt vividly real.

Geography was another window into lands I could scarcely imagine. I could feel the scorching heat of the Australian outback, hear the winds sweeping across New Zealand's Canterbury Plains and taste the rich milk of the dairy farms on England's Salisbury Plains— if only in my mind.

In English literature, I sailed with Captain Long John Silver in *Treasure Island* and journeyed with Gulliver, whose encounters with tiny people reminded me of the imaginary small folk I had once thought lived inside our village radio. Each story pulled me further from the shores of my home into distant lands, planting dreams of far-off places. Mrs Jacka, our English teacher, introduced us to foreign cultures and foods, including the strange fruit called dates—a Middle Eastern staple, as alien to us as cassava or taro might be to others. Then there was Mrs King, our ancient history teacher, who formed a social etiquette club to teach us the proper ways of the *palagi* world. I eagerly joined—not for the enlightenment but for the cakes and tea that accompanied each session. For a hungry boarding boy, this was an opportunity not to be missed!

But it was the sciences and mathematics that ignited my deepest fascination. Chemistry and physics felt like peering behind the curtain of life itself, revealing mysteries I had never even dreamed of. Algebra, calculus and geometry became the tools with which I could unlock the secrets of the universe. The numbers and formulas felt like a new language, a code of logic that could reveal the hidden truths of the world. I soon discovered that I had a natural aptitude for academic discipline—something I had not fully realised before. From that point onward, I was never bested in exams. As I would later learn from Cava Buadromo, the reason the RKS principal had insisted on my transfer to QVS was because of my outstanding performance in the 1959 Secondary School Examination.

I went on to set school records in my final exams— the Cambridge Senior School Certificate and the New Zealand University Entrance Examination—culminating in being named the dux of the school in my final year. These achievements are not mentioned to inflate my ego but rather to reflect the momentum that was steadily building in my life. Each success felt like a victory over my past, a testament that even a village boy from Moala could dream bigger and reach higher.

That is not to say I did not have rivals. Two particularly brilliant students, Yavala Kubuabola, who later became Fiji's Minister of Finance, and Maleli Waqatabua, later the head of the government's IT department, were constant sources of competition. We were great friends, and we pushed each other to excel. Our rivalry kept me sharp and motivated, and I found my own limits stretched because of it.

QVS was not all about academic learning. It was also renowned for its traditions, which played a pivotal role in developing our young minds. Three stood out to me as particularly important. First, there was the annual

debate with the girls' boarding school, Adi Cakobau
School (ACS), culminating in a supervised dance in the
evening. Unsurprisingly, this was the most popular
event, though only senior boys were allowed to take
part. Many lifelong friendships were born during these
youthful exchanges. It also exposed us to forming
opinions on current affairs and matters affecting our
world and our young nation, sharpening our public
speaking skills—qualities that many of my peers later
drew upon as politicians and leaders. Looking back,
I cannot recall a single debate topic, but the rush of
those moments, seeing the curious faces of the ACS
girls, remains unforgettable.

Another highlight was the annual staging of a
Shakespearean play. This tradition did not just involve
the whole school—it captivated the whole country. The
energy and excitement of the crowd, our classmates and
even teachers, became something I looked forward to
each year. We became minor celebrities, especially when
the production went on tour around Viti Levu, even
travelling to Levuka, the old capital, on the island of
Ovalau. Auditioning for roles was fiercely competitive
and, much to my dismay, being top of the class did not
translate into acting talent. I never landed a leading
role, despite my best efforts. However, I soon realised
that even minor parts came with perks—like skipping
prep sessions and weekend chores for rehearsals. From
then on, I aimed for smaller roles, just enough to stay
involved without the pressure of a starring performance.
Of course, there was another reason for my enthusiasm
about the play, but that is a story for later. Most
importantly, this tradition nurtured in us a deep love of
literature, inspiring us to explore other forms such as

poetry. Ha! Poetry. I can see and hear Mr Peacock now coming into the class some days and sitting on his desk to read Longfellow's *The Song of Hiawatha* or *Paul Revere's Ride* or Sir Walter Scott's *Lochinvar*. What music, what rhythm, how transformational!

Lastly, the school made it a priority to teach and preserve our traditional customs. This included traditional dances and the presentation of ceremonial speeches, which is why it was compulsory for each student to bring a traditional club, spear and fan as part of their luggage. These activities kept us connected to our cultural heritage, grounding us in our Fijian identity.

Sports, of course, were always central to our lives, and no boys' boarding school could do without them. Without an outlet for our energy, young boys would surely find other, less wholesome, ways to release it. The legendary rivalry between QVS and RKS lived on, and for many, including myself, this rivalry was personal. As it was at RKS, when I was not on the field, I was an avid cheerleader, passionately supporting my new school. I still felt every loss deeply, especially in rugby, just as I had when cheering for RKS. How fickle loyalty is when you are young!

The annual under-19 rugby final was the crown jewel of this rivalry, often played in Suva's main stadium. The tension in the stands was as intense as the action on the field. I still remember the heartbreak of narrow losses—the sting of defeat that lingered for days, leaving the whole school in mourning. Losing my voice from cheering so much only added insult to injury. Winning was not just about school pride—it became part of our identities and, just as it was at RKS, a badge of honour that could influence future opportunities and reputations.

QVS was grooming us for academic excellence. I may have started out as a village boy but, by the time I left QVS, I would be stepping into the world equipped with knowledge, confidence, and—though I did not know it then—a life full of new opportunities. Those years at QVS moulded more than our minds—they shaped our hearts, gave us purpose and taught us to face the unknown. The journey was not always easy, but with each new subject, each tradition, each game, I could feel myself changing, becoming someone I had never dared to imagine I would become.

CHAPTER 13

BOYS WILL BE BOYS

At QVS, it did not take long for us to find ways to inject some excitement into the rigid structure of school life. No matter how much discipline was drilled into us or how many rules they tried to impose, we were, after all, boys—and boys, as they say, will be boys.

Rules were everywhere, and they were designed to keep us in line. Whether it was about waking up at the crack of dawn, keeping our dorms spotless or attending classes with military precision, there was always someone watching to make sure we stayed in check. But we had our own little moments too—moments like the unspoken, unsupervised contests of how much we could get away with before we got caught. In our minds, for every rule, there was an opportunity—sometimes fleeting, sometimes daring—to infuse a touch of creativity and mischief into our otherwise ordered days. Each small act of mischief while not an outright rebellion, was just a playful testing of the boundaries, a secret sport where we competed to outwit the system, to gain a small victory over the strict structure of boarding school life.

One of my closest partners in crime was my best friend, Pene Tigarea. We had a silent agreement between us—let us see who could go the longest without getting punished for bending the rules. The teachers, of course, were no fools. They knew what we were up to but catching us in the act was another matter entirely. I will never forget Mr Laughlin, one of the stricter teachers, who said to me one day, "I know what you boys are up to. I am going to catch you sooner or later."

With all the bravado of youth, I cheekily replied, "You'll have to catch us first, sir." His narrowed gaze was both a warning and a challenge, but he never did.

That was the game—to push things just far enough without getting caught, to sneak in moments of freedom in a school so tightly controlled. Every victory, no matter how small, was a triumph that we would laugh about later. Whether it was skipping out on a prep session or sneaking some extra time in the dorm after lights-out, we were always testing the limits.

But it was not all about outwitting the teachers. We found adventure in the most unlikely places—like Mr Prasad's peanut and watermelon farm, which just happened to be located right next to the school. Now, I have often wondered who in their right mind would start a fruit farm next to a boarding school full of hungry, energetic boys, but Mr Prasad had either underestimated us or was simply too trusting.

From the moment the fruits or peanuts were in season, it became our secret mission to 'borrow' a few of his crops. This was not theft, at least not in our minds—we were just hungry boys looking for an adventure and maybe a snack or two! The thrill was not just in the eating; it was in the sneaking, the planning and the sense of mischief. We felt like bandits, sneaking out under the cover of darkness, our hearts racing and timing our movements perfectly to avoid detection to claim our share of the 'loot.' The sweet taste of watermelon or the crunch of fresh peanuts never felt so rewarding.

It was not long before I found a way to use the school's Shakespearean play to my advantage. I would always audition for minor parts—small roles that did not demand much time on stage. That was not just because I lacked acting talent (though that was part of it), but because I realised those minor roles gave me plenty of downtime between scenes. They were perfect for slipping away for a quick nighttime raid on Mr Prasad's farm!

There was a cleverness to our pranks, each mischief an art form we perfected. Pene and I would time the gaps between our appearances on stage with military precision, sneaking out of the rehearsal space and over to Mr Prasad's fields. We would return triumphantly clutching our prizes, just in time to rejoin the cast. The watermelon tasted sweeter when shared secretly with friends, the crunch of peanuts a shared victory.

Of course, Mr Prasad was not completely oblivious. He may not have caught us red-handed, but he knew something was up. Perhaps that was why he overcharged us for everything at his shop, where he held a monopoly on school supplies and snacks. In his own way, he made sure he got his due—no one could outsmart him for long. It became a running joke among us that Mr Prasad was getting his "return unto Caesar what is Caesar's" one way or another.

Fruit trees abounded in the vast grounds of the school yet strict rules prohibited us from any unauthorised picking. Of course, this gave us many opportunities for creative mischief. After all, who could not resist the lure of a perfectly ripe mango or the thrill of outwitting a teacher?

Mangoes were, and still are, one of our favourite fruits. One day, Diani, a friend of mine, could not resist the sight of ripe, succulent mangoes hanging just within reach. His stomach overruled his better judgement, and he climbed the tree, ready to feast.

Just as Diani was about to grab a perfectly ripe mango, one of the teachers appeared below. "What are you doing up there, Diani?" the teacher shouted.

Without missing a beat, Diani responded, "Sir, this mango fell onto the ground, and I'm just putting it back on the tree."

I had to admire his quick thinking. Unfortunately, the teacher was not as impressed. Diani was sentenced to two hours of hard labour, cutting grass on his free Saturday afternoon. It seemed a harsh punishment for such a clever excuse. I thought anyone with that kind of chutzpah deserved a reprieve.

Another friend of mine, Niumaia, was a hard nut to crack. It seemed like he spent every Saturday afternoon in detention for one infraction or another. After we watched *Rebel Without a Cause* with James Dean, many of us adopted Dean's signature rebellious look— shirt unbuttoned, collar popped. The school had very strict rules about how shirts were to be worn. Collars had to be neatly folded, and shirts buttoned up to the second-to-top button. But Niumaia was not one to follow rules, especially when they contradicted his newfound James Dean swagger.

One day, as he sauntered down the corridor with his shirt open and collar up, he passed Master Druavesi, one of the school's most feared disciplinarians. Without breaking stride, Master Druavesi barked, "Button up and collar down, my boy!" and kept walking.

Feeling defiant, and certain he was out of the teacher's line of sight, Niumaia gave Master Druavesi a cheeky two-finger salute. What he did not realise was that ahead of Master Druavesi was a glass door that perfectly reflected Niumaia's rude gesture. Without turning around, Master Druavesi raised four fingers behind his back, signalling the four hours of hard labour awaiting Niumaia that weekend. Word quickly spread among the boys—Master Druavesi had eyes in the back of his head!

Of course, I was not above a prank or two myself. One night, I decided to play a trick on my dorm-mate, Bilo, inspired by something I had read in a Hardy Kruger fan magazine. Kruger had once tied a string to his roommate's bed and, in the dead of night, had slowly tugged on it, making his roommate think the bed was haunted. Now, in Fijian culture, we take supernatural things very seriously, and Bilo was no exception.

That evening, I offered to prepare Bilo's bed for him as a friendly gesture. Unbeknownst to him, I tied a thin rope to his sleeping mat and ran it under his bed to my side. When the *lali* drum sounded for bedtime, I could hardly contain my excitement, waiting for the right moment to strike. As soon as Bilo fell asleep and started snoring softly, I began tugging at the string. The snoring stopped. I waited, then tugged again. Silence. After a few more pulls, Bilo suddenly let out a bloodcurdling scream, "Tevoro! Tevoro!" (Ghost! Ghost!) and leapt from his bed, waking up the entire dormitory. I could not stop laughing, though Bilo was less than amused at the time. Years later, when we ran into each other, we had a good laugh about it—thankfully, he forgave me!

Then there was the case of the disappearing peanuts. At one point, I was in charge of the school tuckshop, where we sold peanuts by the scoop. However, I started noticing that the peanut supply was dwindling much faster than expected. It was not until years later that a friend confessed that he and his buddy had discovered where I kept the key to the shop. Every now and then, they would 'borrow' the key, sneak into the tuck shop at night and help themselves to the peanuts. I was just relieved that peanuts were all they had taken—or at least that is all they admitted to!

And then there was the horse incident. David, the principal's son, had a horse he liked to ride around the 205-acre property. Now, I had never ridden a horse in my life, but I had watched plenty of Westerns starring Roy Rogers and Gene Autry. If they could do it, how hard could it be?

One day, David asked me if I could ride. Not wanting to admit my inexperience, I confidently said, "Of course!" I had, after all, learned from the best—on the silver screen! David handed me the reins, and I climbed aboard, eager to show off my 'skills.' With a click of my tongue and a kick to the horse's ribs, just like I had seen in the movies, I urged the horse forward. And forward it went—like a rocket! The freedom was exhilarating until I realised the horse had its own plan. It galloped right across the school grounds and, before I knew it, the horse veered off the path and headed straight for a thicket of bushes. My dreams of being the next Roy Rogers ended in a tangled mess of branches.

But it was not just Mr Prasad's farm or any of the above that provided our entertainment. We were always on the lookout for new ways to challenge ourselves and each other, to turn even the mundane into a test of wits and endurance.

There was a youthful enthusiasm in everything we did, from the smallest act of defiance to the grander schemes that took more planning. We were not just mischievous boys; we were explorers in our own small world, testing boundaries, feeling invincible. Looking back, those days were a constant balance between mischief and adventure. We were not out to cause trouble for the sake of it—we were simply boys looking for a break from the strict routine, pushing the boundaries of what we could get away with.

The thrill of sneaking around, the laughter shared with friends, the unspoken code of brotherhood—it all made school life more than just a rigid schedule of classes and rules. It became a place where every day held the possibility for a new adventure, even if that adventure involved something as simple as a stolen watermelon or dodging Mr Laughlin's watchful eye.

In the end, I think that is what made QVS so unforgettable. It was not just the lessons we learned in the classroom or the rivalries we faced on the rugby field. It was the friendships, the shared moments of rebellion, the youthful daring that made even the strictest rules seem bendable. Boys will be boys, after all—and we were no exception.

CHAPTER 14

A PERSONAL LOSS AND A NEW RESOLVE

In what felt like the blink of an eye, my senior year at QVS arrived, and with it, the looming weight of the Cambridge Senior School Certificate examination. It was 1963, a pivotal year that would determine not only whether I progressed to Form 6 to sit for the New Zealand University Entrance Examination, but also what direction my future would take.

At QVS, no one was allowed to remain at school during the holidays and, by then, I had established a comfortable routine with my mother's first cousin, Qalo, and her husband, Save. They lived in a small, single-room shack with their two boys—no running water, no electricity, but it was a home. Save, a man of quiet strength and unmatched skill with a spear, had a way of turning each fishing trip into a lesson of endurance and resourcefulness. During school breaks, and for hours on end, I would often row the dinghy behind him in Suva Harbour as he dove beneath the waves, spearing fish for us to sell. Once we docked, he would hand me a string of fish bundles with carefully assigned prices, and I would stand at the roadside, straw hat shielding my face, trying to sell the day's catch to passersby.

Standing there for hours, I would pray none of my schoolmates or, worse yet, girls from ACS, would recognise me. Vanity, after all, is never far from a young boy's heart. Save, meanwhile, would often disappear into a nearby pub, leaving me to deal with the fish and customers alone. He trusted I would have sold most of the bundles by the time he returned and, despite my occasional embarrassment, I did my best to help. Helping Save was my way of helping out and a contribution for my board and keep.

It was just before the second school term break when my mother was brought over from Moala to the Colonial War Memorial Hospital in Suva, gravely ill. She was brought in as a medical evacuation, but no one seemed able to explain the seriousness of her condition. I visited her every day during the school holidays, full of naïve optimism. I believed wholeheartedly that the doctors would heal her, and soon she would be back on her feet. There was never any doubt in my mind that she would recover. I was young and, like most boys, I thought tragedy was something that happened to other people.

Even in the hospital room, my mother seemed invincible to me. She would smile and ask about my studies, and I would tell her proudly of all that I was learning. I felt that the connection between us, the strength that had carried us through so much, would help bring her back to health, if only through sheer will.

The day before I returned to school, something stirred inside me, compelling me to visit her once more. Though it was not strictly visiting hours, the staff allowed me to see her. I held her hand as she smiled through her pain. She asked about school, and I told her it was going well. We said a prayer together, her voice soft and weak but steady. As I turned to leave, I glanced back one last time. She had already closed her eyes, slipping back into sleep. I waved, more for myself than for her, as I left the ward, not knowing that this would be the final goodbye.

Returning to QVS, life quickly fell back into its usual rhythm. The focus was now squarely on preparing for the dreaded Cambridge exams. I studied hard, feeling confident as the examination days approached. We completed the last paper, and I breathed a sigh of relief, knowing I had done everything I could. That same day, however, a letter arrived from my brother George. He worked at the Post Office Savings Bank in Suva, and it was rare for him to write to me—so rare, in fact, that as soon as I saw the envelope, a cold dread gripped me. I knew instantly what it was about. He wrote asking me to come and see him before going to Qalo and Save's place.

I refused to let the thought take hold. Denial wrapped itself tightly around me. I convinced myself that the meeting was about something else, anything else. But deep down, I knew. Why else would George write to me now, after all these years of silence?

The holidays arrived and, with a heavy heart, I went to see George at his workplace. As I trudged up the stairs, my feet felt leaden, as if they knew what awaited me. George met me at the door, his face a mask of calm, but his eyes gave away the sorrow behind them. He did not need to say the words. My mother was gone.

I stood there, numb. I wanted to cry, but no tears came. I wanted to wail, but my voice was stuck in my throat. I had prepared myself for this moment, yet the reality hit me like a blow. All the promises I had made to myself—the house I would build for her, the restful old age I would secure for her—evaporated in that instant, leaving behind only emptiness. I had failed her—failed to protect her, failed to give her the comfort she deserved. All the dreams she had encouraged in me felt hollow without her here to witness them, each one a reminder of what I could not give her.

George's voice broke through my fog of grief. "Do you want to stay with me or go back to Qalo and Save?" he asked quietly.

"With you," I replied, barely above a whisper.

And so, during school vacation for the remainder of my schooling, I lived with George in his single rented room, which he generously shared with several homeless boys from the Suva Youth Centre, where he volunteered as assistant secretary. There were six or seven families crammed into this small complex, each occupying a single room, sharing one bathroom and one toilet between them. It was not much, but it was home for the time being. Even for Suva, this was not considered living in poverty, though we often felt we were on the edge.

The rest of the school year passed in a blur. I was impatient to finish, to get on with life, to fulfil the responsibilities I felt weighing heavily on my shoulders. My mother's passing had left a void, but it had also awakened a new resolve within me. Education, I believed, was the key not just for me but for the whole family. If I could succeed, if I could help my siblings pursue their own education, then perhaps we could break the cycle of poverty that had defined so much of our lives.

Her death marked a turning point. In that moment, I grew up. The carefree boy I had once been faded into memory, replaced by a young man determined to take control of his destiny. I still laughed, still enjoyed the company of my friends, but there was a new seriousness beneath it all. Life, I had learned, was fragile—and it was up to me to make the most of mine.

Every success from then on, every challenge overcome, felt as though it was in her honour. This was my new purpose, shaped by the loss that had taken so much from me yet gifted me with the deepest resolve I had ever known.

The year 1964 came and went in a whirlwind. I sat for the New Zealand University Entrance Examination, passed with top grades, and was ready for the Higher Education Course that awaited me in the capital. Yet, despite my newfound resolve, time moved at its own pace. The year was lived fully, with its share of successes and farewells. We won several sports trophies and our production of Shakespeare's *Henry V* was a roaring success. But, beneath the surface, there was a sadness as well, as we prepared to say goodbye to QVS, to the friends we had made and to the life we had known.

For me, though, there was no looking back. My eyes were set firmly on the future, and my heart was full of hope that this next step—this leap into adulthood— would bring with it the fulfilment of all the promises I had made, both to myself and to the memory of my mother, to be a success in whatever I did and to help the family.

That year taught me that life is not only fragile but that with determination and focus, you can transcend this fragility. It taught me that happiness and seriousness can coexist—that you can feel the weight of sadness but still find the strength to rise above it. Friendships can flourish even in the face of loss. Above all, it showed me that when life presents an opportunity, you must seize it without hesitation.

CHAPTER 15

A NEW WORLD: FROM RKS TO COEDUCATION

If I thought 1964 would be the end of new experiences in school life, 1965 at Suva Grammar School proved me wrong, adding yet another vivid thread to the rich tapestry of my education.

Suva Grammar was a world away from what I had known. Back then, it was largely attended by the children of expatriates, sprinkled with those from well-to-do local families. And, unlike the single-gender environment of QVS, Suva Grammar was coeducational—half the students were girls! The transition felt both thrilling and daunting; it was not just a change in demographics but a shift in social dynamics. Apart from my early days at the village primary school, this was the first time I would be studying alongside girls. None of the seven boys who had survived the rigorous academic filtering process at QVS had much experience with this. Now here we were, surrounded by *palagi* children and girls. "Strap yourself in, Joe," I thought to myself, "we're in for a different kind of ride."

Looking back, I now see the logic behind setting up the High Education Course (HEC) year at Suva Grammar. It was designed to expose us to the diversity we would encounter at universities abroad, particularly in New Zealand and Australia. I had grown up with an unspoken belief that *palagis* were superior—our 'betters.' Here, though, I had to interact with them as equals. It was a shift in perspective, and one that would take time to adjust to. If this was a deliberate policy by the powers that be, I applaud their foresight. This was the perfect stepping stone to life overseas.

I quickly saw that, while different, these new classmates were no more gifted than the friends I had known. My previous awe began to shift into understanding; the reality of life was not decided by ethnicity or privilege but by effort and will.

Despite my initial anxieties, those worries soon melted away. Sports, once again, became our bridge into the school's cultural life. As former QVS boys, we were seen as a formidable addition to the school's sports teams, especially in rugby and athletics. Our academic achievements also elevated our status, making us somewhat celebrities rather than outsiders. It was a reverse of my expectations.

Before school began, the Fijian Affairs Board had arranged for us to stay at the Nasinu Teachers Training College, a full boarding college about seven miles from Suva Grammar. They provided us with bus fare allowances to commute to school. At Nasinu, we were treated as guests. Unlike the regimented life of a boarding school, we had no duty rosters, no curfews, and a reserved room for late-night study sessions. We could stay up as late as we liked without adhering to the usual lights-out rules. Even at Suva Grammar School, the requirement to wear school uniforms was relaxed. It was the closest thing to university life we had experienced yet. Freedom tasted sweet.

Then, it was time for day one at Suva Grammar. The anticipation was thick as we gathered for the morning assembly where we were introduced to the rest of the school. I noticed surreptitious glances coming our way, curious eyes sizing us up. We QVS boys were placed in Form 6A, joining other students from various schools. Among them was Donita Simmons from ACS and several students from local Indian and European families. Altogether, we were about fifteen in the HEC class. I mention Donita because, by sheer coincidence, I would reconnect with her 50 years later when she married a friend of mine who moved to Cheltenham, UK, where I now live. Small world indeed!

Back at school, our integration into sports made us popular almost overnight. We turned Suva Grammar into a serious contender in rugby and athletics, and even tried our hand at swimming. That did not last long, though. None of us had swum in a proper pool before; our experience had been limited to splashing around in the sea near our old schools. We also did not have proper swimming trunks or lessons for that matter—only rugby shorts and uncoached natural abilities. One of us who fancied himself a strong swimmer proudly stepped forward for the race. When the race began, his shorts decided they had other plans. He dove in and, when he hit the water, he went in one direction and the shorts went in an entirely different direction! There he was, scrambling to retrieve them, while the rest of us laughed until our sides hurt. It was a moment we would not let him live down for weeks, and it became the stuff of Suva Grammar legend. Amongst us, finding something to laugh at in our adventures—especially at the expense of a fellow QVS boy—was always part of the fun.

Then there was the boys' open 100-metre relay, where our team made up of ex-QVS boys had become the team to beat. We had honed our skills during interschool meets, and our baton changes were practically flawless. Our team included Sakiusa, the first runner, who later became a geography teacher in New Zealand; Maleli, the second runner, destined to be the head of the government IT department; Ratu Isoa Gavidi, the third runner and future ambassador to Australia; and myself as the anchor. We always ran barefoot and trained to perfection, marking the exact spots where each baton handover would occur at full speed, just shy of the disqualification zone.

On the day of the national championship, we were favourites to win. The stakes felt higher than ever, especially since this was our first time competing as part of a coeducational school. The competition extended beyond the track; impressing the girls added a different kind of pressure. As we warmed up, I noticed something unexpected—Ratu Isoa, for the first time, had swapped his bare feet for brand-new running shoes and long white socks. He looked immaculate, like a sprinter straight out of a sports catalogue. Naturally, we teased him mercilessly, accusing him of focusing more on winning the girls than winning the race.

The race began and, as expected, we were leading when the baton reached Ratu Isoa. But then disaster struck. First, the runner from Marist Brothers High School began to close the gap. Second, our perfectly rehearsed timing fell apart. I started my sprint as Ratu Isoa approached our practised handover mark, but as I neared the start of the disqualifications zone, he was still a few strides behind me. Forced to slow down, I turned to see where he was just as he arrived, his spiked shoes slicing into my right foot during the exchange. The baton exchange was clumsy, and though I pushed through the pain and sprinted with everything I had, we finished second. Ratu Isoa's first attempt at running in proper running shoes had slowed him down just enough to upset our well-oiled rhythm.

Afterwards, I was taken to the hospital, my foot bandaged while my teammates attended the post-meet dance. But I had the last laugh. At the next school assembly, the principal singled me out, asking me to stand as he praised my courage for finishing the race despite my injury. Catching Ratu Isoa's eyes, I could not resist a mischievous grin that said it all: "Thanks for the favour. Now guess who the girls are noticing." The friendly rivalry and banter among us never ceased, and moments like these kept our spirits high.

We were young, full of life and determined to make the most of every adventure. There were new dimensions to explore, and we did so with gusto. Each day became an adventure, a discovery of not just people and classes but of the ways we were changing. The very structure of Suva Grammar felt like a world that gave you space to breathe and think beyond tradition and expectation.

In the classroom, I continued to learn valuable lessons—some more practical than others. During one chemistry class, I discovered the difference between ethanol and methanol. Both could cause inebriation, but methanol could also cause blindness and in some cases death. We were at the age where experimenting with alcohol seemed like a rite of passage, but money was always tight. The idea struck me—why not procure a small amount of ethanol from the lab, dilute it with water or juice and get the same effect? This was the reckless brilliance of youth at work (disclaimer: do not try this at home!). I befriended Monty, the lab boy, and secured a modest supply. The experiment worked well enough. However, I noticed my supply always seemed a little smaller than expected when I retrieved it from its hiding place back at Nasinu. Years later, my good friends Ratu Isoa Gavidi and Viliame Cavubati (VC to us) confessed they had been helping themselves to my stash. We laughed about it—though, in hindsight, I am glad they saved me from any more dangerous experiments!

As the year wore on, the moment we had all been waiting for—the advertisement for scholarship applications—drew closer. It felt as if time slowed down, the anticipation making the wait feel endless. But finally, it arrived, and all of us in Form 6A eagerly applied. This was it—the gateway to the future we had been working towards.

Filling out the application forms felt like the closing chapter of one journey and the start of another. I could not help but reflect on everything that had brought me to this moment—the challenges, the hard work, the friends made along the way, the unshakeable determination that had carried me through and my personal loss. Life had thrown its share of obstacles in my path, but I had learned that, with determination, anything was possible.

CHAPTER 16

THE INTERVIEW—CROSSROADS TO THE FUTURE

I received a letter that required me to attend an interview at the Government Education Department office in Suva. The date and time were clearly stated, and it felt like the culmination of everything I had been working towards.

That morning, I showered, dressed in my best clothes and a pair of sandals, and made my way to the office. I was directed to a waiting room and told to wait until my name was called. It was nerve-wracking. "Why is my shirt wet?" I wondered. Then the answer came: "It's perspiration, silly." "Why are you perspiring?" I asked myself. "Because you're nervous!" On went my internal dialogue, a tug-of-war between nerves and reassurance.

It struck me then how, after all those years of schooling and tests, no one had ever taught us how to handle an interview. We were trained to excel in exams, memorise facts and uphold discipline, but this—facing a panel, selling ourselves—felt like uncharted waters. It seemed like an oversight now that I was sitting there nervous and unprepared. How useful it would have been to know the basics—the dos and the don'ts, how to present ourselves and how to answer the difficult questions that might come our way. Or to have been told, for instance, to look the interviewer in the eye rather than look at the floor as was the Fijian custom of subservience to authority. But it was too late for regrets. In that little room, I decided to just be myself, to answer honestly and without trying to second-guess what they wanted to hear. I did not know what they wanted anyway, so why take the risk?

After what felt like an eternity, my name was called out. I stepped into the interview room, and the atmosphere was immediately intimidating. It was a large, wood-panelled office, with four people seated in a semicircle around a coffee table. Directly opposite them, a chair awaited me. I was ushered to it and sat down, feeling dwarfed by the grand room and the serious faces.

There were two *palagis* I did not recognise, along with the Secretary for Education, Semesa Sikivou, and the Secretary for Fijian Affairs, Josevata Kamikamica—an imposing panel if ever there was one. And then there was me: a boy from the village sitting in front of these giants of authority, trying to hide the butterflies in my stomach.

I had been specific in my application, stating that I wanted to study electrical engineering—a rare choice among Fijian boys at the time. Most would not have known the difference between the various branches of engineering, let alone selected one with such confidence. So, naturally, the very first question was, "Why do you want to study electrical engineering?"

Without hesitation, I told them the story of the electric iron from all those years ago at RKS—the shock I had received out of sheer curiosity and my vow to understand the mystery behind it. As I spoke, I could see a shift in their expressions—from formal detachment to genuine amusement and interest. Somehow this almost childish tale became my foundation, a symbol of everything I had pursued without fully realising it. As I recounted the story, they laughed, and the tension in the room lifted. In that moment, I knew I had them. The rest of the interview passed in a blur.

A week later, I received a letter notifying me that I had been awarded the top scholarship to study electrical engineering at the University of New South Wales in Sydney. The scholarship was granted by the Australian Government, the only one of its kind in Fiji at the time. It was part of the Commonwealth Fellowship Plan Scheme, similar to the Colombo Plan Scholarship Scheme for students from Asia.

What followed was a whirlwind of preparations. My brother George and I scrambled to get everything in order. With no prior experience of travelling overseas, we were navigating uncharted territory. It felt both thrilling and overwhelming—how could we know exactly what I would need for a future I had never seen? There was no guidance on what to pack or what to expect. We relied on guesswork and common sense. I remember George's one firm piece of advice: "Don't buy narrow-toed shoes. Your feet are not made for those. You've been barefoot for 19 years, and those shoes will only give you blisters." He was right, of course. Sensible shoes would save me from a lot of pain. I did not forget to pack my sleeping straw mat (woven for me by my sister Sera) and my trusted cane knife. It was just another trip, and this was what we always did. They were our constant travelling companions, familiar links to home.

1965 was a year to remember. Farewells were said. I collected my tickets from the Australian High Commission, along with instructions about what to expect upon arrival at Mascot Airport in Sydney. It was all happening so fast—in my excitement, I barely had time to reflect. I was swept up in the flurry of activity, too busy living in the moment to think too deeply about what lay ahead.

But now, as I write this, I can see what that moment truly was. It was the culmination of my long journey through school—through all the triumphs, trials and tragedies. It marked the end of one chapter of my life and the beginning of another. I was leaving behind the world of village simplicity, the warmth and familiarity of the life I had known, from the world of *bures* and shared floors with my siblings and friends and stepping into a world so foreign that I wondered if I would recognise myself on the other side.

I was moving towards a life of urban sophistication and academic discovery, one that would take me far beyond the familiar shores of Fiji. It was a leap into the unknown, into what people called the forefront of civilisation. All I could feel was excitement—a sense of anticipation for the adventure that lay ahead.

CHAPTER 17

WINGS OF WONDER—MY FIRST FLIGHT TO SYDNEY

And what an adventure it was! It all began with my very first visit to an airport, and not just any airport, but the bustling Nadi International Airport. Until then, I had never been in one. The sheer size of the runway stretched out before me, so vast it felt like it could span two villages back in Moala. Then I saw it—the Boeing 707 coming into land. The roar of the engines shook me to my core though, in reality, it was only my imagination running wild. I thought back to Waqa Avenisi's old description of cars as "big pigs with glaring eyes." But this... this was something far beyond anything I had ever seen. It could have swallowed a few of those pigs whole, and now, I was about to step into one. The sight of it stirred excitement and terror.

What would it be like inside? I would soon find out.

After clearing customs, the call to board came. I followed the crowd, trying to take in every moment, hoping to recall this experience vividly one day, perhaps to my grandchildren. Here is what it was like.

I felt like a boy standing at the edge of a vast, unknown ocean, ready to dive in but not knowing what lay beneath the surface. You, in this modern day, are probably far more familiar with airplanes than I was back then. Today's passenger jet planes are much bigger, much faster. But imagine, just for a moment, being called to board a spaceship bound for the moon. Imagine your heart racing with excitement at being chosen, feeling weightless even before liftoff. That was me. Every step towards the plane felt monumental, as if I were leaving one world behind and stepping into another.

In my eagerness, I almost tripped over the last step. Inside, the plane was even more magnificent than I had imagined. Waqa Avenisi's 'big pig' had turned into an enormously big bird—powerful, streamlined, somehow light enough to fly but large enough to hold all of us. The sheer ingenuity of it left me in awe. This was not just a machine—it was a symbol of what humans could achieve when they dreamed beyond the possible. How does it fly? How can it carry all these people and their luggage? And how on earth do you steer such a thing? Questions spun in my mind.

Once inside, I was shown to my seat. The seats were neat, stylish and inviting. "Settling in" was hardly the right phrase to describe my state of mind. I was a bundle of nervous energy, excited beyond belief but also quietly terrified. Would it take off? What if something went wrong? You could not exactly pull into a repair shop mid-air! My imagination, vivid as ever, was not making this first flight any easier. But the thrill of the unknown drowned out my fears.

Then came the announcement: "Fasten your seatbelts." The engines hummed and roared as we taxied along the tarmac. The greenery outside the window became a blur—and suddenly we were airborne. Looking down at the town of Nadi from the sky, the realisation hit me. I was really on my way to Sydney.

The rest of the flight passed in a daze of blue skies and endless ocean, though it was not without its surprises. When lunchtime arrived, I was startled by the array of utensils placed in front of me. Back home, one spoon was all you ever needed. But here? There were multiple forks, spoons and knives. Mrs. King's social etiquette lessons at QVS had not covered this! Fortunately, I watched the passenger next to me, mimicking his every move until I made it through the meal unscathed. He was, without knowing it, my silent tutor that day.

Then came the pilot's voice over the intercom: "We'll be flying over Botany Bay shortly. Look to your left, and you'll see Sydney." My heart raced. There it was—Sydney!

But my first glimpse of this legendary city was... underwhelming. As we flew over rows and rows of suburban bungalows, I could not help but feel a pang of disappointment. Where were the towering skyscrapers I had seen in magazines? This looked just like a much larger version of Suva. I had expected everyone in Sydney to live in skyscrapers. It was not until later that I understood the difference between the central business district and the suburbs. I had arrived with expectations shaped by glossy photos and film—glamorous visions of a glittering skyline—but here was a city far more complex and sprawling than I could have imagined.

After clearing customs, I stepped into the vastness of Sydney's airport. If I had thought Nadi was big, this was a whole new world. Endless corridors, planes landing and taking off in every direction, and a constant hum of activity that buzzed like nothing I had ever experienced.

The city life I had only read about in books seemed to start right here at the airport.

I was greeted by Miss Chamberlain, the liaison officer, holding a placard with my name on it. She whisked me away in a Commonwealth car to the Bondi Pacific Hotel, overlooking the iconic Bondi Beach, where I would stay until university began. Bondi Beach! I had never heard of it before that moment, but the sight of the ocean stretching out beneath the skyline was strangely comforting. I was a world away from the simple life in Fiji.

That first night, standing at the window of my hotel room and gazing across the beach and beyond to the Pacific Ocean, homesickness hit me like a wave. I thought of my mother, of everything we had been through. The emotions that I had kept at bay finally surfaced and, for the first time since her passing, I broke down. I cried for everything—for her, for the life we never got to share, for the dreams I would never be able to fulfil for her. It was a release I had not allowed myself until that very moment. Coming from a deeply religious family, I prayed to God that, as I could not provide for her in this world, I would carry all her sins, if any, into the next. Then, as was the usual Fijian boarding school custom, I spread my straw mat on the already made bed and went to sleep. What must the cleaning person have thought the next morning!

When morning came, I woke to the sunlight streaming through the window. I showered, dressed and went downstairs to breakfast. There, I discovered I was not the only student staying at the hotel. Several Asian students on Colombo Scholarships were also there, and we were scheduled for a bus tour of the city.

As we toured, Sydney unfolded before me. The first day, I finally saw the towering skyscrapers I had expected, their glass facades gleaming in the sunlight, making the city feel alive and buzzing. We visited the Commonwealth Office, and I took my first-ever ride in an elevator. Each new experience came at me quickly, but I marvelled quietly, taking it all in.

On the second day, we were taken to lunch in an underground restaurant. *Underground!* The very thought of dining beneath the surface of the earth was astonishing. In Fiji, digging a hole usually meant dealing with water before long, but here? They had entire floors bustling with people and business below the city streets, as if they had tamed the elements themselves. The ingenuity of it all left me amazed at how these *palagis* seemed to defy nature's limits.

And just as I thought I had seen it all, the next day brought another shock—an underground train system! The idea of trains crisscrossing beneath the city, weaving their way through tunnels below towering skyscrapers, was beyond anything I could have imagined. These tunnels, these miles of track beneath me, these huge trains crossing endlessly below the earth—it felt like entering a hidden, magical city!

One awe-inspiring discovery followed another. As if these marvels were not enough to truly blow a village boy's mind, we were soon taken across the iconic Sydney Harbour Bridge—the one I had only ever seen in glossy magazine photos. Seeing it up close was something else entirely. This massive structure, carrying eight lanes of traffic and even a rail line, spanned a vast stretch of water with such grace and strength that it seemed to defy all logic.

Of course, if you grew up in Sydney or any modern city where such things are part of everyday life, you might ask, "What's the big deal?" But if you walked in my shoes—coming from a village where the horizon was defined by the ocean and the tallest buildings barely coconut-trees height—you would understand my astonishment, excitement, bewilderment and my awe all wrapped into one. Sydney was opening a whole new world for me, and each moment left me in wonder.

That week of exploration was much more than just sightseeing. It was both a process of acculturation—a glimpse into what life in this vast, modern city would be like—and a transformation—a journey from the village boy I had been to the person I was becoming. I enjoyed it until it was time to part ways with my fellow students and settle into the university's residential college.

CHAPTER 18

FRESH STARTS, CULTURAL STUMBLES—
NAVIGATING COLLEGE LIFE

University orientation week is a universal tradition, a rite of passage for students stepping into the next chapter of their academic lives. At the University of New South Wales (UNSW), it was no different. The week was packed with activities designed to help new students settle in, make friends and find their way around campus. But when you were a "fresher" at a residential college in Australia, this tradition took on a different twist, one filled with unexpected and, at times, unpleasant surprises. That is where I was heading— Philip Baxter College, a place where orientation meant something quite distinct.

I checked out of the Bondi Pacific Hotel, caught a taxi and arrived at Philip Baxter College with a mixture of excitement and trepidation coursing through me. Why the nerves? I had been pre-warned by a fellow Fijian student, Viliame Gonelevu, about what to expect. His parting advice was simple but invaluable: "Wear socks to bed during orientation week and tuck some money into them." I did not understand what this meant at the time, but it would not take long to find out.

On my very first night, I was jolted awake by loud banging on my door around 2 a.m. A group of senior students, grinning like mischievous demons, told me to get dressed and follow them. I quickly pulled on my socks—making sure my hidden money was still in there—and followed them outside. Two other freshers were already waiting in a car. Pillowcases were pulled over our heads, and we were driven off into the chilly night. Eventually, the car stopped, and we were let out one by one. I was the second. They handed me a five-cent coin and told me to find a public phone booth and use the money to call for help if I got lost. Then, they sped off, leaving me standing alone in the middle of a quiet, unfamiliar neighbourhood.

It was only my second week in Sydney, and I had no clue where I was. The cold was biting, much harsher than anything I had experienced in Fiji. "Steady, Joe. Take stock," I muttered, forcing calm into my voice even as panic loomed. The only sensible option was to head towards the nearest lights and hope to find a phone booth or, by some miracle, a taxi. After what felt like an eternity of walking through eerily empty streets, I saw another figure approaching. To my relief, it was a fellow fresher who had also been abandoned by the seniors.

Together, we pooled our resources—our five-cent coins and the extra cash I had hidden in my socks. We eventually found a phone booth, called a taxi and made it back to the college, exhausted but relieved. However, our ordeal did not end there. The next night, we were dragged out again, forced to run to Coogee Beach (a six-kilometre sprint), fill pillowcases with sand and haul them back to build sandcastles beneath the windows of the freshettes. As if that was not humiliating enough, they were instructed to dump buckets of cold water on us from their balconies. The 'pranks' escalated until, on his birthday, one poor fresher was dumped half-naked into the El Alamein Fountain in Kings Cross and told to find his way back to campus. Fortunately, he had the good sense to approach the police, who returned him to the college in one of their vans.

After a few more pranks, I had reached my limit. I was ready when the inevitable banging came at my door; I had rigged a bucket of water above it. The seniors got a soaking when they barged in. After a few choice expletives, they realised I was not playing their game anymore. "Do what you want," I told them. "But I'm done with these childish pranks." Surprisingly, they left me alone after that.

Thus began my university life, though not without a few cultural missteps along the way.

University itself was a new frontier—a sprawling, vibrant institution where it was easy to feel like just another face in the crowd. Yet, within the halls of Philip Baxter College, I found a sense of belonging, a community that softened the enormity of campus life. The camaraderie fostered through team sports like rugby, cricket and athletics created bonds that extended beyond the field. Rugby, in particular, became my gateway to friendships, drawing me into a close-knit group that felt more like family.

Among those early friendships, two stood out: Iain Couper and Peter Done. Through shared victories, defeats and countless memories on and off the field, these two mates became lifelong friends, the kind who remain constants through life's changes.

But the connections I formed extended beyond the rugby pitch and the college quad. University life offered the chance to meet remarkable individuals from all walks of life and some friendships, forged in that unique environment, would stand the test of time. Two such friends, Jane Schwager and Janice Kaplan, became dear companions whose support and kindness enriched my university years and continued to do so long after. Their friendship was a testament to the deeper bonds that can grow when people meet at pivotal moments in their lives, when they are just beginning to carve out their paths in the world.

But as much as I loved playing rugby, it occasionally led me into trouble. After our last exam of the year, a few of us, riding high on the relief of being done, decided to celebrate with drinks in Kings Cross, the city's red-light district. After a night of revelry, two of these university classmates (Hugh and Jeevens) and I began an impromptu game of touch rugby down a side street. It was not long before a police car pulled up, and we were arrested for disorderly conduct. Hugh, being under 18, was released, while Jeevens and I were taken to a holding cell. Jeevens had some money on him and was able to bail himself out. I had nothing.

To my embarrassment, Jeevens returned to college and announced in front of a full recreation room that he was taking up a collection for my bail. Thankfully, the Dean of the college, Professor George, stepped in and topped up the funds, allowing me to return to college that same night. The next day, a student wit had tipped off the editor of the college newspaper, and the headline read, "FIJIAN RUGBY PLAYER ARRESTED IN KINGS CROSS." I had earned notoriety in the last way I had ever wanted! But it gave my fellow students something to talk about for weeks.

There was another tradition at the college that I was not prepared for—formal dinners from Monday to Thursday. The dress code was strict: academic gowns, mortar boards, jackets, and ties were mandatory. While I had no trouble acquiring the required gown and mortar board, my idea of 'formal attire' was... let us say, flexible. In Fiji, 'formal' meant any shirt, tie, jacket and a comfortable pair of footwear, flip-flops included. Proper shoes had never been a priority.

For an entire term, I attended these formal dinners in colourful Hawaiian shirts, ties, jackets, academic gowns, mortar board on my head and flip-flops, blissfully unaware of the cultural faux pas I was committing. I must have looked like an eccentric tourist trying to blend into a school choir. It was not until rugby season started, and I got to know Iain better and vice versa, that he pulled me aside and said, "Joe, mate, you've got to stop wearing your pyjamas to formal dinner. And you need proper shoes." Mortified yet grateful, I quickly learned the importance of a closed-toe shoe and a plain business shirt.

Despite my blunders, university life proceeded smoothly. I was doing well academically, and the Commonwealth Office liaison, Miss Chamberlain, regularly checked in to make sure everything was going well. The process of settling into this new culture seemed to be going smoothly—until the college ball. Billed as a 'black-tie affair,' I assumed this meant a smart jacket, literally a black tie, and any shoes. How wrong I was. When I arrived with my date, I quickly realised that 'black tie' was far more formal than I had imagined. My casual attire (but with a black necktie, mind) stood out like a sore thumb. Peter, seeing my discomfort, took me aside, filled me with enough drinks to numb the embarrassment, and explained the true meaning of 'black tie.' Mrs. King's etiquette lessons had not gone far enough!

University life was not confined to the campus. There was a thriving Pacific Islander community in Sydney and, once a month, we gathered for a 'Pacific night' by the waterfront—a lively event filled with Pacific music, dancing and food from home. It was a chance to reconnect with other Fijians, especially the boys from QVS, and share stories from our school days.

It was during one of these Pacific nights that I found myself in another memorable situation. A beautiful Hawaiian dancer was performing the *tamure*, a traditional Pacific Island dance and, as custom dictated, she selected a male from the audience to join her after the formal part of the floor show. Unbeknownst to me, Gonelevu had pointed her in my direction. Suddenly, I was her partner! Fortified by a few drinks and armed with some knowledge of the dance, I managed to hold my own. To everyone's surprise, including the dancer's, I did well enough that her manager approached me afterward, offering $25 and a free meal if I would perform with her every Saturday night at his restaurant. How could I refuse? I was an accidental performer and much the envy of the other Fijian Students!

By my third year, I moved out of college and shared a flat with another Fijian student, George Tavanavanua. I also bought a little Honda 50cc scooter, but learning to ride it was a series of painful lessons. Having never ridden a bicycle, let alone a motorbike, I crashed twice before I could stay upright. Even when I earned my licence, navigating Sydney's traffic proved to be another challenge. I had two more accidents that landed me in the hospital for observation, leading my friends to joke that if I did not turn up after rugby games, they should call the hospital first.

To supplement my scholarship, I took on a part-time cleaning job. I had to pay $15 for cleaning training and certification before I could land one, but it was worth it. Years later, I would jokingly tell my staff that I had a degree in industrial cleaning—and I had the certificate to prove it!

All too soon, my university studies came to an end, culminating in the proud achievement of being awarded my degree in electrical engineering. Looking back to my eleven-year-old self, standing in the RKS ironing shed and wondering about that electric shock, I could hardly believe how far that spark of curiosity had carried me. The moment had arrived and I was ready to step into the world and earn a living. Yet, perhaps the greater triumph was the personal transformation that had unfolded within me. Immersed in the vibrant cauldron of multinationalities and multiethnicities that defined university life, I finally shed the weight of my old inferiority complex about being of mixed heritage. In embracing my roots, I discovered a profound strength—a blend of Fijian warmth and gregariousness fused with Chinese resilience and work ethic. Together, these traits formed a unique identity, enabling me to transcend racial barriers with confidence and pride. It was as though, for the first time, I truly saw myself for who I was and who I could be.

CHAPTER 19

BUILDING A FAMILY AMID DISASTERS

There was always a clear understanding that if you received a scholarship, you were expected to return to Fiji after your studies to contribute to the country. I wholeheartedly agreed with this but, being in Australia, it felt like a missed opportunity to not gain some practical experience before heading back. Australia offered a scope of opportunities that Fiji simply could not. I wrote to my prospective employer in Fiji, the Fiji Electricity Authority (FEA), requesting a short secondment to Australia. They agreed and arranged for me to spend nine months with the Sydney County Council for experience in electricity distribution, followed by another nine months with the New South Wales Electricity Commission for hands-on experience in electricity generation.

With everything arranged, I began my first full-time job, diving headfirst into the world of professional engineering. Meanwhile, I had met a wonderful girl named Gillian Gregory, whom I had been dating since university. We were serious and, in 1972, we got married and prepared for the next big adventure—moving to Fiji. But before we made the move, life threw us a beautiful surprise: Jill was pregnant with our first child. The joy of expecting our first child was indescribable—a heady blend of excitement and responsibility, a wonder

KAI JAINA: A WORLD BETWEEN

we had never felt before. We were creating something uniquely ours, a life born out of love.

So, we sailed to Fiji on a cargo passenger ship, a five-day journey through the boundless Pacific. As the ship cut through the waters, my thoughts were filled with the anticipation of becoming a father, mixed with nostalgia. I was returning home, but this time with a new family and a puppy dog in tow.

Until now, my experiences had focused on adapting from my Fijian way of life to a Western one, but Jill was now facing the reverse process. Shy, reserved and very much a private person, Jill was suddenly thrust into the boisterous, warm, and communal world of Fijian culture. As was the custom, we moved in temporarily with my brother George and his family upon our arrival in Suva.

Jill's culture shock must have been immense. We were living in a two-bedroom flat shared with my brother, his wife Ani, their three children, Ani's in-laws, and two cousins. Every inch of space seemed alive with movement and chatter. My family did their best to make her feel welcome, but they too were unsure how to navigate this new dynamic. Privacy, which Jill had grown up with, was suddenly a luxury she did not have. The sharing of facilities, the constant hum of family conversations, a new language and the unfamiliar taste of Fijian food must have added to her sense of disorientation. Yet, despite her discomfort, Jill bore it all with quiet grace and she never once complained, silently bearing the challenges. I admired her deeply for her strength.

Meanwhile, I was tasked with finding us a home. My job with FEA was based in Lautoka, a city on the dry, sun-baked western side of Viti Levu, over 200 kilometres from Suva. After two weeks of searching, I secured a rental—a sprawling colonial-style wooden house perched on a hill overlooking the sea. Seeing Jill's face as we moved in was a moment of pure relief. The house offered her what she had been missing most—space, privacy and the calming view of the ocean. It was a far cry from the crowded chaos of Suva. The rudimentary kerosene stove for cooking did not seem to bother her and, for the first time since our move, we felt truly settled.

Then, about a month later, disaster struck.

I was at work one morning when a uniformed fire officer came to inform me that our house had burned to the ground. My heart leapt to my throat. Fear gripped me. Was Jill all right? Was the baby all right? I rushed home, frantic, only to learn that Jill had escaped unscathed, but our home was gone. The fire had started with the kerosene stove. Jill, unfamiliar with its workings, had inadvertently caused the blaze. We lost everything: all our belongings, our wedding photos, important papers, and even our beloved puppy. It was a devastating blow, an emotional upheaval atop an already challenging time.

But out of the ashes came something beautiful: friendship and community. My fellow old boys from QVS rallied around us, led by none other than Viliame Gonelevu, the same friend who had advised me during my college orientation. Friends from college and Sydney also sent clothes and essentials to help us rebuild. For the next few weeks, we lived a nomadic life, moving from one old boy's home to another until we could find a more permanent place to stay. Once again, Jill showed immense resilience. Despite the upheaval and carrying our unborn child, she remained composed, never faltering.

Eventually, we found a house to rent, and slowly we rebuilt our lives. Our new home had a serene, neighbourly atmosphere, with a New Zealand couple, Mark and Ann Clapham, living next door, and another QVS old boy, Ratu Osea, living nearby with his Australian wife, Lyn. With the baby's due date approaching, life started to feel more settled. Jill made friends, and we began to feel at home once more.

It turns out that babies cannot be planned—they come when they are ready. Our daughter, Sera, was due towards the end of August, but the end of August came and went. It was a nerve-wracking wait, each day filled with anticipation. Then, on the morning of 1 September, just as I had left to deal with a fault at a power station in Sigatoka, Jill went into labour. A call came through from the FEA, informing me that she had been rushed to the Ba Methodist Mission Hospital. I turned the car around and dashed across the island, arriving just in time to meet my beautiful baby girl.

Holding Sera in my arms for the first time was a feeling beyond words—a moment of sheer wonder. After everything we had been through, here she was, perfect and healthy, a miracle in every sense of the word. Jill had carried her through all the turmoil, and now we had our little girl. Jill's mother, Margery, also came to visit—an important moment for Jill, as Margery had initially opposed our marriage. Seeing them together felt like a quiet triumph over the struggles we had faced. Margery's presence was a gesture of acceptance, a bridge mending the distance that had once seemed so vast.

Just as we began to settle into life with our newborn, fate decided to test us once more. In October, Cyclone Bebe hit Fiji with devastating force—the strongest hurricane in 20 years. With wind speeds of over 100 mph, our home was battered. The roof was ripped clean off, leaving us once again without shelter. This time, it was not fire but the rage of nature itself testing us. Afterwards, it was like a temporary campsite living in the house while repairs were being carried out by our landlord. But each promise our landlord made and did not fulfil, and each completed section finished to dubious standards or each shift in the completion date, deepened our frustration. The instability wore on us but, thankfully, relief came when one of FEA's vacant quarters became available. After some negotiations, we were finally able to move in, trading chaos for a semblance of stability. For the first time in months, there was a sense of calm—a space that allowed us to breathe again and begin rebuilding what had been shaken.

Two years later, in August 1974, our second daughter, Tracey, came into the world, her arrival at Lautoka Hospital filling our hearts with a familiar yet uniquely wondrous joy. Each child's birth felt like a reaffirmation of life's beauty, a miraculous gift that carried its own story. Jill's time carrying Tracey had been mercifully smooth, a contrast to the challenges she had faced during Sera's arrival. Knowing the strength it had taken Jill to endure previously, I felt an overwhelming gratitude for the blessing of an easy birth. With Tracey, our family of four was complete—a perfect balance of love and promise for the future.

While our time in Lautoka had its challenges, it also brought joy and friendships. Some of the happiest memories were made on camping trips with friends to Natadola Beach—a breathtaking, untouched stretch of coastline that, years later, would become a famed tourist destination and golf resort. But, back then, it was a pristine natural haven where Jill and I watched our little girls playing and laughing with the waves lapping at their feet, free of any care in the world. Moments like these felt like gifts, memories we would cherish for a lifetime.

Life in Lautoka also brought some much-needed humour. I reconnected with my old schoolmate, Viliame Cavubati, or VC as we called him and yes, it was the VC who with Ratu Isoa used to pinch my ethanol supply all those years ago. A larger-than-life character, VC was as irrepressible as ever. One New Year's Eve, we both found ourselves at the Fiji Sugar Mill Club in Ba, completely skint—we had no money for drinks. VC, always quick on his feet, came up with a plan.

"Don't worry, Joe," he said, his eyes gleaming with mischief. "I've got this." He hopped up onto the stage and made an announcement that nearly made me faint. He declared that we would perform a *vakamalolo*, a traditional sit-down dance from our school days. Horrified, I told him I had forgotten how to do it.

"Just follow my lead," he whispered. "They're too drunk to notice anything!" and so, we performed. To our surprise, it was a hit, and we were not allowed to pay for another drink the rest of the night. VC's irrepressible spirit had saved the day once again, and we laughed about it for years to come.

Through the trials and triumphs, the missteps and miracles, life had thrown plenty at us. But Jill and I faced each challenge side by side, strength garnered through shared determination. And, with friends like VC, we always managed to find a way to laugh through it all.

CHAPTER 20

NEW BEGINNINGS IN SUVA—FROM SETBACKS TO SUCCESS

While there were always challenges, both at work and in life, overall, our time in Lautoka had been fulfilling. Yet, as the years passed, I noticed a growing restlessness in Jill. It was understandable—Lautoka, at that time, was not exactly a thriving cultural hub. Compared to Suva, it felt like a backwater. Most of Jill's friends were expatriates, and the turnover of people was constant. Just as friendships were made, they would move on to their next postings elsewhere, leaving behind another round of farewells. For someone like Jill, who found it hard enough to form new friendships in an unfamiliar environment, the regular partings took an emotional toll. It was not easy for her, and I was acutely aware of it. I could feel her quiet yearning for a more dynamic environment, a place where her friendships would not dissolve with every new expatriate departure.

One day, Jill came to me with an idea. She showed me a position advertised in the local newspaper—Operations Officer for Shell Southwest Pacific Islands, based in Suva and reporting to Shell Pacific Island Holdings within Shell Australia. The company covered operations in Fiji, Tonga, Western and American Samoa, the Cook Islands and Niue. This was the kind of opportunity that could lead to further advancement, possibly even back to Australia. I had never seriously entertained the thought of leaving Fiji as my sense of loyalty and commitment to my home country were very strong. Nevertheless, I could not deny that a move to Suva would make Jill happier. It would also provide better schooling options for our daughters and a welcome increase in salary, along with company housing.

So, I applied for the job and, to my surprise, was offered the position. In October 1975, we packed up and moved once again—this time from one side of Viti Levu to the other, from the dust and heat of Lautoka to the green, vibrant capital of Suva.

We had weathered so many storms, both literal and metaphorical, during our time in Lautoka. The fire that destroyed our first home, the hurricane that tore the roof off our second, and the challenges of raising a young family in what was for Jill a foreign land had tested us in ways we never expected. Yet, despite the difficulties, we had fond memories too. Lautoka had been a place of resilience, learning to rebuild and thrive in adversity, a proving ground for our determination. But this phase of our journey had come to an end, and now we were ready to embrace the next chapter.

Suva was a breath of fresh air and greeted us like a long-awaited embrace. The lush greenery and cooler humid climate immediately lifted our spirits. Unlike Lautoka, with its dusty stillness and scorching heat, Suva was alive with activity and a pulse of energy of its own. As the nation's capital, it was the cultural and arts centre of Fiji, and there was always something happening. Jill, the girls and I settled in quickly. The sadness of leaving

Lautoka was replaced by a sense of renewal as we discovered the vibrancy of Suva. I started my new job with Shell, and the change invigorated me.

One of Jill's greatest loves was horses. Whether it was riding, training or simply being around them, horses brought her joy. Fortunately, there was a pony club in Suva. Before long, we had acquired two ponies, and I was elected chairman of the club. Jill seemed to flourish in this environment, teaching our daughters how to ride and helping other young girls in the club. She even broke in one of the ponies herself, something she took great pride in. I felt the move to Suva had been the right decision. Our family was thriving, and the disasters of the past seemed to fade into distant memories.

But, as life had taught me time and again, challenges often lurk around the corner.

Three months into my new role, disaster struck again—this time, at work. Both the General Manager, Tom Millard, and the Operations Manager were in Melbourne for a conference, leaving the Administration Manager in charge. It was a day like any other—a typical tropical downpour—when one of our fully loaded fuel trucks overturned, caught fire and tragically killed both the driver and the fitter who had been travelling with him. Our acting GM was overwhelmed and uncertain of what to do. Sensing the urgency, I stepped in, taking charge of the situation without hesitation.

I gathered one of our supervisors, Harry Rounds, and I drove to the accident site. The scene was horrific, but there was no time to dwell on that. My thoughts were with the families and the immediate needs—we needed to take the right steps in the correct order. In the pouring rain, amid the chaos, I found clarity in action—coordinating emergency services, visiting the grieving families on behalf of the company according to traditional protocols, arranging for the bodies to be transported to their families in Lautoka and ensuring the company provided immediate financial assistance. I then had to face the inevitable press, and by the time Tom Millard returned two days later, I had already written up a full report on the incident.

Little did I know that my actions had made a lasting impression. Two weeks later, a letter arrived from the Chairman of Shell Australia—a moment of bittersweet pride, the commendation a stark reminder of the tragedy that had earned it.

Despite the sad event, I was beginning to learn the ins and outs of the oil industry. The faster pace and performance-driven nature of the private sector suited me, and I found the work deeply satisfying. I was fortunate to have Tom Millard as my boss—he was an inspiring leader and a mentor who believed in me. He saw the potential for local leadership within the company, and I suspect he had me in mind as a future candidate for the general manager role. Through his mentorship, I learned not just about the oil business but also about what it took to lead.

Under his guidance, I flourished, and after two years with Shell, I was promoted to Operations Manager following a brief training stint in Australia.

At home, the girls were growing up fast and blossomed in Suva's nurturing environment. They began attending an international school, and I watched with pride as they developed their own personalities. Sera, sensitive and gifted, earned early praise from her first teacher, Mrs Yarrow, for her quiet intellect. Tracey, on the other hand, was fiercely independent. Her first full sentence was "I can by myself," a phrase that became family lore and her mantra, one that defined her determined spirit. Jill, meanwhile, secured a position at the National Training Institute as a psychologist. Our life in Suva felt settled, stable and full of promise, even as I sensed Jill's quiet yearning to return to Australia—a place that still held part of her heart, it seemed.

Nevertheless, just when everything seemed on track, a conversation with the Islands Manager from Shell Australia, Stuart Keane, seemed to throw Jill a lifeline and made me re-evaluate my future. During his tour of the Pacific, he asked me directly where I saw myself in the years to come. It was a question that took me by surprise, as I had not given it much thought. But I could not tell him that, so I responded honestly:

"I would like to be good enough to become General Manager here, but I don't think that will be possible without further experience in a larger market, like Shell Australia. Unfortunately, as a non-Australian, getting a position there would be difficult due to visa restrictions. So, I'll probably give this position another two years then consider moving into a government role in Fiji."

A month later, as if fate were eavesdropping, an offer arrived from Shell Australia, a position waiting for me in Melbourne and instructions to apply for a visa at the Australian High Commission. It felt like the universe had conspired with fate to offer us a lifeline that seemed to bridge Jill's yearning and my professional aspirations. And so, at the beginning of 1980, our visas came through. Once again, we packed up, said goodbye to friends and family and prepared to move—this time, back to Australia.

As the plane lifted off, I looked at Jill, who seemed happier and more hopeful than I had seen in years. In her eyes, a quiet radiance spoke to the homecoming she had longed for. For me, it was a step forward, carrying the lessons and trials of Fiji in my heart, ready to embrace whatever lay ahead.

CHAPTER 21

MELBOURNE—DREAMS
AND THE SEPARATION

We had never lived in Melbourne before, and settling in took time. The city itself was vast, sprawling and vibrant, with a population of around three million back then. Its suburbs seemed to stretch on endlessly—80 kilometres from north to south and 60 kilometres from east to west. It was easy to feel lost, both physically and emotionally, in a city of that size. Yet, its vastness and its unfamiliar pace felt both exhilarating and overwhelming, like stepping into a kaleidoscope of opportunity and isolation. In those early days, Melbourne felt like a place where I sensed we could start anew.

Even in 1980, it had all the makings of a world-class city—diverse cultures, cuisines from every corner of the globe and an air of cosmopolitan sophistication. The charm of Melbourne began to seep into me; its changing seasons, the wide green parks and the genuine warmth of Melburnians were both welcoming and comforting. In fact, Melbourne would later go on to be named the "Most Liveable City in the World" for seven consecutive years from 2011 to 2017. It felt like a place where one could belong. For the first time since leaving Fiji, I thought to myself, "If we were to settle anywhere, this would be the city." I was hopeful that Jill would feel the same way and that we could make Melbourne our home.

Our first priority was finding a place to live, somewhere suitable for the family and the girls to start school. Within the first month, we found a home in the semi-rural suburb of Chirnside Park, at the northeastern edge of Melbourne's suburban sprawl, 38 kilometres from the city centre. With the help of Shell, we made our first-ever down payment on a house—a huge commitment for us. The train ride into the city for work was long, but the area was peaceful, surrounded by nature, and we thought it would be perfect for Jill's love of horses. She soon found a place nearby to indulge her passion and, for a time, it seemed like the move to Melbourne might just give us all a fresh start.

But things do not always go as planned. While Jill found solace in her horses, our daughters struggled at school. Like me in my village days, they faced the cruelty of children who targeted anyone different. Our girls were different—not only were they new arrivals, but their olive skin set them apart. Australia had only recently dismantled its discriminatory 'whites only' immigration policy and, while the law had changed, the attitudes had not fully caught up outside the more urban areas.

The girls never told me about the bullying they faced; they bore it in silence, much like I had all those years ago. It was not until years later that I learned of their struggles and, even now, thinking back to that time, my heart aches for the two little girls who endured such torment without sharing it. I wish I could have protected them from the pain. But, like me, they bore the weight of prejudice in stoic silence and, I believe, it made them stronger in the end.

Despite their troubles at school, there were bright spots. Our neighbours were friendly, and one family even had a swimming pool that our daughters would visit. The friendships they made with the neighbour's daughter brought some relief, and I hoped it might ease the difficulties they faced at school. Jill accepted a job as the manager of a nursing agency, and she seemed happy. It felt like we were settling into a new way of life, this time in a big, modern city in Australia.

As for me, I was doing well at work—perhaps too well. My role had me travelling all over Australia, visiting Shell depots and terminals in cities and remote towns alike. I crossed the continent, north to south and east to west, learning just how vast and diverse Australia really was. I met incredible characters along the way and, through them, I began to understand the Australian way—dry humour, a sense of mateship and an unwavering commitment to doing the right thing. But the demands of the job brought an unexpected cost. My work, once the anchor of our stability, had become a wedge—its demands pulled me further from Jill and the daughters I so desperately wanted to protect but found myself drifting away from.

Almost two years into our life in Melbourne, Jill told me she wanted to move again. This time, she was drawn to a small 15-acre farm in Trentham, a country town 110 kilometres from the city. It felt like an attempt to reclaim something lost between us. I saw the move as an opportunity to reconnect, to bring back a closeness that had slipped away with the busyness of city life. Determined, I offered to help Jill with breaking in a new pony we had acquired, a gesture to mend some fences and reconnect.

Breaking in a pony, I would soon find, was far from my usual skill set. My experience with horses, after all, was confined to the big screen and memories from school days. Jill had done all the groundwork with the pony—getting it used to being saddled and managing the saddle's weight. Next came the final step: having someone mounted while being walked gently around the training ring, letting the pony get used to a rider. Thinking I would impress her, and in the spirit of mending fences, I volunteered to be the rider. To my surprise, it went well at first, and we circled the ring smoothly a few times.

Then, out of nowhere, the pony stopped abruptly. Unaware that ponies often pause for nature's call, I nudged her with my heel, attempting to mimic the cowboys I had seen on screen. That gentle nudge was all it took—the pony leapt forward, her ears back, my control slipping. We hurtled towards the fence and, in an instant, she swerved, leaving me suspended in the air. I crashed into the fence ungracefully. Mending fences indeed! The gods seemed to have their own idea about that, but the irony was not lost on me. I limped away with a bruised body and ego while Jill tried her best not to laugh.

What I did not see coming, however, was the bombshell that followed this move. Jill wanted a separation. Her words, simple yet devastating, shattered the illusion of stability to which I had clung. The request felt like stepping into a void, a place where everything familiar dissolved into uncertainty.

I was blindsided. I had not noticed the cracks forming in our relationship but, looking back now, the signs were there. My constant travel, the hours spent immersed in work, the lack of shared interests—all of it had driven a wedge between us. Slowly, imperceptibly, we had grown apart. I tried to change her mind, tried to show her that I still cared, but her mind was made up and she was resolute—the quiet erosion of shared dreams had created a chasm too wide to bridge.

For a while, I lived in a motel during the week, returning to the farm on weekends, but it was not the same. We were like strangers. I felt helpless, as if everything I held dear was just out of reach, slipping further from my grasp each day. My heart ached, not only for what we were losing but for what our daughters were going through. The thought of being separated from them was unbearable, but we were caught in a whirlwind that neither of us could seem to stop.

Amid the chaos of our separation, an unexpected offer came from Shell. They wanted to promote me to Operations Manager for Shell in Papua New Guinea. It was a chance to move forward in my career, but it meant uprooting our lives again, this time to Port Moresby. Jill was adamant that she did not want to go and, as our separation loomed larger, it became clear that it would be a permanent one. Perhaps the distance would give us both the space we needed. Maybe, I thought, absence would indeed make the heart grow fonder, though part of me feared it would only confirm the distance already between us.

With a heavy heart, I accepted the offer. In February 1982, just two years after arriving in Melbourne, I left once more—this time for Port Moresby, but without my family. The memory of that morning remains vivid, etched in my mind like a snapshot of heartbreak.

As I stepped out the front door in the stillness of the early hours to make my way to the airport, little dearest Sera slipped a note into the palm of my left hand. In her sweet, childlike handwriting, she wished me a good trip, told me how much she loved me and how deeply she would miss me. It was a gesture so tender and heart-wrenching that it stopped me in my tracks. In my already fragile state of mind, the weight of her words and the purity of her love brought tears to my eyes. Quiet tears slid down my face on the way to the airport, a testament to the depth of my bond with my children and the ache of leaving them behind.

I kept that note. It has stayed with me through the decades, folded and refolded countless times, a tangible connection to a moment of innocence and love that has outlived the years. Just recently, over 40 years later, I had the privilege of reading it back to Sera in Australia, her words as poignant now as they were then, her love as enduring as ever.

As the plane took off and the Melbourne skyline receded into the horizon, a heavy sense of loss settled over me. It felt as though a part of me had been left behind with my family, with the life I was leaving. I stared out at the city, its lights fading into the distance, and wondered if I would ever find my way back—to the familiar comforts of home, to the precious moments of love and laughter that now seemed so far away. The journey ahead was uncertain, but in that moment, my heart was tethered firmly to the life I was leaving, a life I already missed more than words could convey.

CHAPTER 22

PAPUA NEW GUINEA—EMBRACING THE WILD AND LETTING GO

Papua New Guinea in 1982 was a place unlike any other—a place where the ancient and the modern collided, creating a kaleidoscope of untamed beauty and formidable challenges. It was fiercely alive, chaotic and filled with a rich complexity that drew me in even as it kept me on edge. For such a small country, PNG boasted a staggering seven hundred languages and countless tribal cultures, each with its own customs and way of life. Its people carried a unique, almost primal, strength, each tribe fiercely independent in thought and behaviour with a pride that ran deep. A modern state on the surface, PNG was still cradled by thick tropical forests, some of the world's deepest caves and most diverse fauna and flora, and remote villages where life remained close to nature, as it had been for centuries. In the Highlands, tribes still lived in grass huts, walked around carrying bows and arrows and wearing grass skirts, unbothered by or unaware of the Western notions of propriety. The contrast was mesmerising, a blend of ancient traditions within the fringes of modern civilisation. I was immediately captivated. It was wild, and it was raw. PNG's intensity was magnetic—a mix of beauty, danger and mystery that left me feeling both awestruck and cautious.

Alongside its vibrancy, PNG had its dangers—both natural and human-made. The cities, and particularly Port Moresby, had become magnets for a fast-growing population drawn from the rural areas, but the pace and customs of city life clashed with tribal beliefs. Young men, disconnected from the structures of village life, formed gangs, and crime, especially break-ins and burglaries, was rampant. 'Rascal' gangs roamed Port Moresby with little regard for Western laws, and human lives for that matter, often taking what they wanted and retaliating against anyone who resisted. The local tradition of 'payback' made violence an accepted response; if one life were lost, even by accident, it was customary to take another in retribution. In the early 1980s, curfews and even martial law were necessary to curb crime, but the tension remained in the city.

At my Shell briefing, vigilance was stressed over valour: "If you're burgled, surrender what they want; resistance invites retribution. And if you accidentally hit a pig with your car, drive immediately to the nearest police station—it's not just livestock; it's livelihood and sacred to many." For many of the indigenous, taking a life is simply part of the payback custom, and pigs were among their most treasured possessions, often treated like family members. They would fiercely protect them, even breastfeed the piglets as though they were their own. Losing one could provoke intense retaliation.

Meanwhile, Port Moresby felt like a city under siege, with homes encased in six-foot-high barbed-wire fences and doors and windows fortified with steel bars. Knowing these risks, I was relieved that my family was not with me. Life here required constant vigilance, and the thought of raising the girls here was unsettling. For all its palpable risks, PNG exuded an allure that was difficult to resist—a chaotic symphony of danger and wonder whose spirit was a lodestone. So, despite the chaos, and once being burgled, I felt the pull of the place and was ready to be part of it.

Arriving at Port Moresby's International Airport, I was struck by the red stains on the walls and sidewalks. My boss, Alan Krebs, who met me at the airport, explained that they were from betel nut juice. Betel nut, a mild stimulant chewed daily by locals, was a ubiquitous sight in PNG—its juice staining walls, teeth and concrete in streaks of bright red. Seeing it was disorienting at first but reinforced my sense that I was somewhere very different. Checking into the Port Moresby Travelodge Hotel, I was relieved to find pristine walls and clean paths, a stark contrast to the streets.

I spent my first two weeks shadowing my predecessor, Robert Grigg, who was wrapping up his term. We travelled through remote towns, met terminal and depot managers across the country and eventually reached the Solomon Islands, which fell under our jurisdiction. The journey was like a masterclass on PNG's landscapes and diverse cultures; each place we visited felt like another world. I was particularly struck by the warmth of our indigenous managers. For them, seeing a fellow Pacific Islander in this role sparked a natural warmth, a kindred spirit as though I was a bridge between their world and Shell's. After Robert returned to Australia, I knew that the friendships I had started to form would help me find my footing here. Robert also left me his dog, Suzie, and a cat named Turi, whose company brought me comfort in my first days alone. Suzie had a local reputation for riding Ela Beach's waves with windsurfers, something I admired as I adjusted to my new reality.

On my own, I revisited each terminal manager to establish my presence. Travelling with my guitar as a companion, I quickly became known as "the guitar-toting Operations Manager," a symbol of my approachability and Pacific Island roots. Despite the dangers, the wildness and my own solitude, I began to feel connected to PNG in ways I had not anticipated.

Only two months into this chapter of my life, however, the past returned to haunt me. Jill contacted me to initiate divorce proceedings on grounds of irreconcilable differences. I had felt it coming, yet its finality landed like a blow. It marked the conclusion of a chapter I had long hoped could be rewritten. We had tried to build a family and create a life, but now it all seemed to have dissolved before me. I did not contest the divorce; all I asked for was unrestricted access to the girls and to keep my favourite rocking chair. She agreed and, just like that, our years together were over. Family had been my foundation, my central identity—and now that foundation had seemingly vanished.

Work had once been my sanctuary, but now it merely amplified the emptiness. The vastness of PNG's mountains and forests seemed to mirror the desolation I felt within, each remote outpost a reminder of how far I was from the life I had known. My very existence was a constant reminder of the life I had worked so hard to build yet failed to hold on to. I took up golf and tennis, anything that would keep me busy after hours. My daughters' letters became treasured lifelines, their words and little stories piercing the emptiness that followed me around.

And yet, despite these moments of emptiness, life in PNG was not all shadow. Through sports and work, I began forming connections that became meaningful as I settled further into this unexpected chapter. Amid the solitude, the wonders of PNG started to feel like a new home. I began to see that, like PNG itself, life could be wild, unpredictable and still worth embracing. It was an unfamiliar life, unlike anything I had imagined, but it was my life, and I was determined to find a way forward within it.

CHAPTER 23

NEW BEGINNINGS AND FINDING SARAH

When the final decree nisi of my divorce came through, the reality settled in. I had already been living with the truth for some time, but seeing it finalised on paper stirred something deeper. In those quiet hours, with too much time on my hands, I could not help but re-examine my life to that point. What could I have done better? Was it all preventable? These questions loomed, and I started to see that the reasons for our separation were cumulative—like steady drops of water wearing away at the stone of marriage. Over time, these differences, largely rooted in cultural clashes, had eroded the foundation. It became clear that if there were ever a 'next time', I would need someone who understood these complexities, ideally someone who shared a similar background and values.

Work continued to present its challenges, especially in the unique cultural context of PNG. There were different values and expectations at play, and it was clear that the indigenous workforce often balanced traditional roles with workplace demands. One story stood out to me: an Australian manager had invested time in mentoring a young local man to manage the Honiara oil terminal in the Solomon Islands, only to find the local man had left to return to his village by the beach. The manager tried to reason with him, saying, "One day, you can retire with good money, build a house, and enjoy the beach just as you are now." But the irony was palpable. It reminded me of how 'success' in the Western sense held little weight in a culture that valued family and immediate happiness over distant goals.

As for me, work in PNG was as intense as ever, with projects underway and management changes to navigate. Despite the bustle, there were quiet evenings when I felt the loss of my daughters acutely. But the finality of the divorce nudged me to accept things as they were and to move on. It was time to embrace change, even if it meant navigating uncharted emotional terrain.

Soon enough, we needed a planning manager in our Sales and Marketing department, which was led by my Dutch colleague George Dikker-Hupkes. We received several applications, but one CV stood out. The applicant had been an analyst with the Group Planning Department at Shell's head office in London and was travelling through PNG with plans to stay a while. George and the General Manager, Alan, were keen on her experience, and I agreed to sit on the interview panel. However, I had reservations. PNG could be a harsh, even unforgiving place, and I wondered if a single woman would be prepared for its unique environment.

On the day of the interview, she did not arrive, nor did we hear from her. We assumed she had moved on, and I could see George's disappointment. But later that day, the personnel manager tracked her down. She had been caught in a flood in a remote village and could not contact us, managing only to find her way back to Port Moresby by hitching a ride in a dugout canoe then a single-engine plane. That tenacity quieted my concerns about her resilience. Here was someone who, despite overwhelming challenges, had returned undeterred—a spirit not easily intimidated.

We rescheduled her interview, but I was called to the Highlands and sent my deputy, Gerry Phipps, in my place. Later, Gerry called to say she had been offered the position and was set to start in a week. "Her name is Sarah—young, blonde, beautiful—but I am not sure how well she will handle Port Moresby," said Gerry, echoing my concern.

When Sarah started, she met with George, who would be her immediate boss, and I decided to introduce myself. Gerry's description had been apt—Sarah had a calm beauty about her, the kind that could have been at odds with the gritty reality of PNG. I could not help but wonder what had brought her here, to a place where few Westerners would venture so freely. She seemed delicate and poised, yet her return from the flooded village hinted at an inner strength I had not yet understood.

Some weeks later, Gerry and I took her to lunch at the Papua Hotel as a token of welcome from our department. Eager to learn more about her, we peppered her with questions, and she responded thoughtfully. With a degree in science, she had begun her career with Shell in London as a planning analyst and was later sponsored by Shell for an MBA at the London Business School. After being introduced to the Baha'i Faith by a Shell friend, she had subsequently become deeply involved in it, joining a call to support the Indigenous Baha'i community in PNG, which was why she had been in a remote village when the flood struck. Her journey, driven by faith and a commitment to service, left a lasting impression on me. To leave a promising career in London and come to PNG out of commitment to her faith and community required courage and conviction. The more I observed Sarah, the more I admired her, not just for her skills but also for her dedication and quiet strength.

As we worked together, Sarah and I grew closer. She was diligent and highly capable, but she balanced her professional excellence with an unshakeable dedication to her Baha'i Faith, spending weekends in distant villages to serve and connect with indigenous communities despite the obvious dangers. Her dedication moved me. It resonated with my own values. Though I felt tempted to ask her out, my recent divorce had left me cautious, wary of becoming close to another Western woman only to face disappointment again. Still, as the weeks passed, my hesitation faded. Observing how completely at ease she was with the Indigenous people and how the villagers seemed drawn to her natural warmth, I reminded myself of my vow to move on and open a new door. Gathering my nerve, I finally asked her to dinner. The evening was wonderful, filled with warm conversation, yet it took a serious turn when Sarah looked at me and said plainly, "Joe, the most important thing in my life is my faith. It matters more than any relationship we may or may not have."

Her candour startled me as it was refreshing. Her faith was clearly integral to her life, and I reminded myself not to be flippant about it. I respected her even more for her clarity and her unwavering sense of purpose. As we got to know each other, our connection deepened, and a genuine friendship grew. Even so, I was cautious, though my interest in her grew daily.

Eventually, her contract with Shell ended, and she took a new role as an economist with the PNG Government. Our bond remained strong despite our busy lives. Then, in

September 1984, I received an unexpected recall to Melbourne. This pleased me very much because it meant that I was able to see Sera and Tracey regularly. However, leaving Sarah behind was harder than I anticipated. Soon after arriving in Melbourne, I realised I could not let her slip away. One evening, unable to ignore the growing certainty in my heart, I called her. My voice steady but my heart racing, I asked her to marry me. The pause that followed felt infinite until her gentle 'yes' turned the moment into one of life's rare and profound joys.

She joined me in Melbourne after fulfilling her contract. Her mother, her only surviving parent, gave the required permission, while I, with no surviving parents, had only my own decision to make. We therefore prepared the arrangements for our union with great respect for her Baha'i Faith. Then, on her birthday, 27 February 1985, we were married by a Baha'i marriage celebrant in the beautiful Fitzroy Gardens with a few close friends and my two daughters in attendance. We celebrated over lunch at the nearby Hilton Hotel and, just like that, we began our life together. It was a simple beginning to a life that has, since that day, been rich in every way. With Sarah, I felt I had found not only love but a true partnership, a meeting of values and purpose.

There was one more task I had to complete, though: I wanted Sarah to meet my family and experience my village in Fiji. It was important to me to share this part of my heritage, although having watched her with the villagers in PNG, I did not think I had anything to worry about. I arranged a family gathering in the village, inviting siblings who had long moved away, so it could feel like a homecoming. Traditions dictated that we collect gifts for the village, and we shipped these ahead of our arrival—drums of kerosene, bolts of cloth, non-perishable food and other essentials to benefit the family and the community. I had also planned donations for the village and church funds, hoping to make our visit a meaningful one.

Finally, the day came. We flew to Fiji and, with my siblings and extended family, we travelled to the village. For three days, we celebrated with traditional gatherings and ceremonies. There was the welcoming ceremony, offerings of the gifts we had brought, and a moving homage to those who had passed in our absence. I watched, heartened, as Sarah took part in these serious rituals, gliding through the ceremonies with a serene respect that won over everyone. She underwent traditional dances and rituals customary for a foreign bride, but it was her genuine openness that endeared her to my family. Watching her bond so naturally with them, embracing the village traditions and its rhythms with genuine respect, and seeing their reciprocated warmth towards her, I saw in her a partner not just for life but for the journey of bridging two worlds. I knew I had made the right choice. Whatever differences lay between us, they felt less like obstacles and more like parts of a whole. With that comforting thought, we returned to Melbourne. With quiet certainty, I felt I had found someone who would stand by my side, understanding the world I came from and the life we would build together.

CHAPTER 24

DREAMS REALISED AND A NEW LIFE IN FIJI

As I progressed through Shell, my conversation with Stuart Keane years ago, when I first dared to dream of leading Shell in the Southwest Pacific region, became a guiding light. That dream never faded—each challenge and promotion a step closer to realising that dream. After some years of effort, I sensed that, if it were meant to be, the opportunity might finally be on the horizon. My supervisors' assessments had consistently praised my performance, and I felt prepared to take on the role. Meanwhile, Sarah had rejoined Shell once again, this time working with Shell Chemicals, whose office was conveniently located next door to mine. We had bought an apartment in East St Kilda, and life started to take on a semblance of stability, particularly with regular visits from my daughters, who were now blossoming into young women.

Renewing my relationship with my daughters was something I had longed for, although I was aware that their relationship with Sarah was still delicate—a natural result of the complexities surrounding our blended family. We tried to bridge the gap with humour and family moments. Our family outings were punctuated with light-hearted antics—me, the self-proclaimed rooster among my brood of hens, crowing theatrically to their adolescent mortification, while Sarah and I laughed ourselves breathless at their flustered attempts to dodge attention. As the girls reached their teenage years, they quickly learn to read my mind and to hide among the shoppers to avoid my antics. Little by little, these moments helped to ease the tension and added fond memories to our family folklore.

Then, three and a half years after our return from PNG, I was finally offered the job I had long dreamed of—General Manager of Shell Fiji Ltd, overseeing the Southwest Pacific Islands region. There was nostalgia as I thought of those who had contributed to this journey. Jill, who had first encouraged me to apply for Shell; Tom Millard, my first boss, who believed in my potential and urged me to think beyond Fiji; and Stuart Keane, who, with that pivotal question, prompted me to articulate my goals. They had all moved on—Tom and Stuart had retired, and Jill and I were divorced—but their impact on my life remained. I accepted the offer, even though it meant that Sarah would have to leave Shell for the third time. Fortunately, we were both ready for a new chapter that included the possibility of starting our own family, a hope we shared deeply.

In March 1988, we arrived in Fiji. The country was grappling with the aftershocks of its first military coup. Sitiveni Rabuka was now in control, and the country was in economic straits as a result of his coup. Many organisations, including the government and military, struggled to pay their bills. Repeated demands for the government to pay their significant outstanding debt had been ignored. One of my first tasks, therefore, was to resolve these overdue payments to stabilise our cash flow—a task resolved not through standard channels but by a direct call to Rabuka, an old QVS junior. Thanks to our old school ties, we had a warm conversation, and he quickly agreed to settle the debt, allowing us to move forward without issue.

Settling into life in Fiji was seamless. Sarah quickly made friends, became active in the local Baha'i community and even began learning the Fijian language. I felt as though I had never left. Reconnecting with my homeland, especially in the presence of family, gave me a renewed sense of purpose and belonging. My daughters Sera and Tracey visited us every main school holiday, and our new home soon filled with the joys of family life. Unemployment in Fiji was high—to help ease this situation, Sarah and I hired two housekeepers. The laughter and camaraderie shared among Sarah and our housekeepers brought a familial warmth to our home that felt uniquely Fijian. Amid the laughter and amity, I sometimes could not help but wonder if they ever got any work done!

A few months after our arrival, we received wonderful news—Sarah was expecting! On 21 March 1989, our daughter, Lina, was born. Given that Sarah was over thirty and healthcare resources in Fiji were limited, her doctor had advised us to consider an overseas delivery. We flew to Cheltenham, England, where Sarah's mother, Lina, lived. Our daughter was named after her grandmother, a nod to Fijian tradition. Cradling Lina for the first time was transcendent, and experiencing the raw beauty of bringing new life into the world was magical, a deeply cherished moment that made me feel the power of family anew. I proudly accepted the midwife's offer to cut the umbilical cord, an experience I had missed with my older daughters due to traditional customs. This moment was one of raw connection transcending anything I had experienced before.

After a month in England, we returned to Fiji, stopping in Vancouver to visit Sarah's brother, Steve, on the way.

Once home, our housekeeper Emele embraced her role with an even deeper sense of love and care, helping Sarah with everything and doting on baby Lina. The bond between them grew, and Emele became more than a helper—she was family. Her gentle care and kindness reminded me of my family back in the village.

In those early years, some of my happiest memories were of Lina's little feet pattering across the wooden floor, her voice calling "Daddy, daddy" as she ran to greet me after a long day. Sometimes, on family walks, her legs would tire, and she would raise her little arms, calling out "uppie", which was her way of asking to be lifted onto my shoulders.

Lina was also born with an innate sense of mischief and mystery, traits that filled our lives with joy and wonder. One day, when she was just three years old, she was playing alone on the floor of our house, laughing softly to herself. Curious, Sarah asked what had made her laugh so much. Without missing a beat, Lina replied with a calm nonchalance that only a child could muster: "I was sharing a joke with God." It was a moment that left us both astonished and deeply moved, a glimpse into the unfathomable depth of a child's world—a world where the extraordinary felt perfectly natural.

Sarah's Fijian language lessons progressed well and, one day, she suggested that she might like to try giving a speech in Fijian at a public event. I had recently received an invitation to be the guest of honour at QVS for their annual inter-house athletic competition, and I proposed that Sarah take my place. The principal was delighted. She would be not only the first Western woman but the first-ever woman to do so and, in the Fijian vernacular to boot. The challenge energised Sarah, who worked tirelessly with a Fijian tutor to perfect her speech. She was committed to making a meaningful impression. On the day of the event, standing in front of 400 students, dignitaries and old boys, including the Deputy Prime Minister, Sarah confidently began her speech in Fijian.

"I am honoured and very happy to be here amongst you to present the prizes for your athletic competition," she said in Fijian. However, instead of saying *veitau cici* (athletic competition), she mistakenly placed emphasis on the wrong syllable, turning *cici* (to run) into a word meaning something else entirely. The result? She had inadvertently congratulated the students on their farting competition.

For a moment, the air was thick with barely contained laughter from the boys and polite nudges from the dignitaries beside me, implying deliberate intention on my part. Sarah, thinking she had done wonderfully, basked in the chuckles she assumed were signs of appreciation. On the drive home, I could no longer hold it in and told her what had happened. After her initial shock, she laughed until tears streamed down her face the entire way back. Later, when she recounted the story to Emele, our kind-hearted housekeeper, Emele slid down the wall in fits of laughter, wiping tears from her eyes. Watching Emele, a traditionally built lady, sink down the wall in slow motion remains one of the most unforgettable images of my time in Fiji. Sarah took the lesson to heart, vowing never again to deliver a speech in another language without a final practice session with a native speaker.

But there was an unexpected denouement to this story. Years later, when we were transferred to Brisbane,

I received a call from a fellow QVS old boy, Aca Soqosoqo. He asked if I could extend a helping hand to his son Alex, who was coming to Brisbane with his young child for a rare medical treatment available only in Australia. Without hesitation, I agreed.

Alex and his wife (who could not come immediately as she had to stay with their child) were invited to dinner at our home. I introduced Alex to Sarah when he arrived. In typical Fijian custom, he bowed his head respectfully, avoiding eye contact, and said shyly, "I have met your wife before." Intrigued, Sarah asked where. Alex, still looking downward, admitted with a sheepish smile, "I was the head boy at QVS and was introduced to you at your 'famous' athletics prize-giving speech... in the Fijian vernacular."

In an instant, we burst into spontaneous laughter, Sarah joining in as she remembered the moment fondly— her infamous faux pas of mispronouncing a key word and transforming "athletic competition" into "farting competition." The memory, brought back so unexpectedly, turned our dinner into an evening filled with shared hilarity and connection. Even years later, the story continued to live on, a testament to the enduring charm of Sarah's willingness to embrace her husband's culture and to laugh at life's missteps.

On the professional front, I was equally happy. As the political landscape in Fiji stabilised, the newly elected civilian government recognised the desperate need for indigenous Fijians to participate more fully in commerce. They established Fijian Holdings Ltd as a vehicle for this purpose, and I was honoured when the Finance Minister, Josevata Kamikamica, invited me to serve on its board. It was an opportunity to give back to my country in a way that felt meaningful, a small step towards fostering economic inclusion for indigenous Fijians.

The invitation carried even greater significance because it came from Mr. Kamikamica, a man I deeply respected for his unwavering integrity, steadfast conviction and enduring commitment to Fiji. There was an air of assurance about him—a quiet strength that inspired confidence and the courage to stand firm for his values and what was right. Serving under his guidance was not only a professional privilege but also a deeply personal honour. He was also, by sheer coincidence, one of the members of the Commonwealth Fellowship Scholarship interview panel who interviewed me and subsequently endorsed me all those years ago. He was, to me, a role model.

The work with Fijian Holdings Ltd was immensely satisfying. The company thrived under a shared vision of empowering indigenous Fijians, ultimately becoming one of the nation's most successful businesses. Even now, as I write these words, its success is a testament to Mr. Kamikamica as one of those rare leaders who truly embodied the ideals of visionary leadership—a reminder of the impact one person's values can have on a community and a nation.

Around this time, I built a holiday home in my village, creating an emotional anchor and a bridge linking my present and my past. It was a place where Sarah, Lina and I, and occasionally Sera and Tracey, could visit to reconnect with village friends and relatives. These family visits were joyous gatherings, filled with the laughter and chatter of my siblings and their families. Each visit became a celebration, a vibrant tableau of family, tradition and enduring bonds that stretched across the years and distances. My siblings had each charted their own paths, and I often thought of my mother during these times, wondering what she would have thought of all we had become.

I also became actively involved in the QVS Old Boys' Association, rekindling the bonds of brotherhood that had shaped so much of my youth. Dusting off my cricket skills, I joined the old boys' team in the local league. Much to the chagrin of our captain Filimone Jitoko, what began as a competitive endeavour quickly transformed into lively social matches. These gatherings extended well beyond the boundary lines, bringing families together for picnic-style afternoons under the warm Fijian sun. Sarah and (after Lina was born) with Lina would bring sandwiches, watermelons and other treats, turning each game into a festive family affair. It was not just about the sport; it was about laughter, camaraderie, family and the joy of shared moments. Sometimes, it felt as if time itself slowed down to let us savour these idyllic days.

It was during one of these sun-drenched afternoons, as the sounds of cheerful banter echoed around me, that I had a rather mischievous idea: to combine two of my most beloved institutions—my village and my school— in a one-of-a-kind cricket match. The proposal was met with immediate enthusiasm, spreading through the Old Boys like wildfire. Soon, the plan had taken on a life of its own. Influential Old Boys sprang into action: a boat was hired, traditional gifts for the village were organized and a list of players and contributions towards the trip began to take shape. My message to the village chief, who happened to be my brother-in-law, Ratu Nacanieli Draunidalo, was met with equal excitement. For the villagers, this was an event of historic significance—a chance to host the alumni of a school they revered as the pinnacle of Fijian achievement.

An elder of the QVS Old Boys' Association was appointed to lead our contingent, none other than the then Minister of Education, Filipe Bole. It was a fitting choice, though we all knew it would also make him a prime target for the light-hearted mischief that was sure to come. You see, Filipe hailed from Vanua Balavu, whose people share a tau-vu (traditional kinship) relationship with my island, Moala. This connection meant that he was fair game for endless teasing and harmless trickery—a fact he was well aware of and braced for with good humour.

The much-anticipated day arrived, and the atmosphere at the wharf was one of excitement. Despite our best efforts to limit numbers, the Old Boys turned out in droves. We could have fielded four cricket teams with enough left over for reserves! Knowing this would be a "boys' three nights out" affair, our partners wisely and good-naturedly stayed behind. All except Sarah, who was six months pregnant with Lina. Determined to reconnect with my relatives, especially my sister Sera. Sarah declared, "I wouldn't miss it for the world."

Her bold declaration raised more than a few eyebrows, most memorably from Elisapeci, Filipe's wife. Sidling up to Sarah on the wharf, she asked with a wry smile, "You aren't going with them, are you?"—a comment that, loosely translated, meant, "Don't tell me you're brave enough to travel with these reprobates!" Sarah, unfazed, repeated her declaration with equal humour, "I wouldn't miss it for the world," fully aware of what Elisapeci was implying. As I helped my heavily pregnant wife up the gangplank, I could not help but feel the significance of this moment—bringing together two of the most important worlds of my life.

Our arrival in the village was nothing short of monumental. The villagers welcomed us with the full splendour of Fijian tradition, exchanging gifts and hosting a feast that was legendary in its variety and abundance. For them, the QVS Old Boys represented an institution that had produced some of Fiji's greatest leaders, and this event would surely be recorded in village lore. The kava flowed freely, and our players spent most of the night in animated conversation, much to the delight of our hosts. Meanwhile, unbeknownst to us, the village players had been sent to bed early—a strategic move, as we were soon to discover.

The next morning, the match began under a set of peculiar local rules. For instance, players could not be dismissed on the first ball and, if a bat flew out of a player's hands and was caught, they would be declared out. As hosts, the villagers also reserved the right to decide who batted first—and of course, our leader Filipe, was made the opening batsman.

Filipe strode to the crease with all the grandeur of a cricketing legend. Dressed immaculately in pristine whites, he waved to the crowd like royalty, soaking in the cheers and playful jeers from the tau-vu spectators. As the bowler prepared to deliver the first ball, a group of village women suddenly rushed onto the field. Armed with bottles of coconut oil and talcum powder, they proceeded to drench Filipe in oil and dust him liberally with powder, rendering his glasses nearly opaque and his hands slippery beyond repair. The crowd erupted in laughter and Filipe, now thoroughly transformed into a comical figure, gamely took his stance.

The bowler charged in, and Filipe executed a picture-perfect cover drive. The ball sailed harmlessly past to the wicketkeeper but, his bat, slick with oil, spun high into the air. The crowd watched in stunned silence as it somersaulted before being caught by a mid-on fielder. "Out!" declared the village umpire with mock authority, prompting an explosion of laughter from players and spectators alike. From that moment on, the game descended into a joyous farce, filled with hilarity and good-natured antics.

Three days later, we returned to Suva, our boat heavy with laughter, goodwill and unforgettable memories. Who won the game? It did not matter. What mattered was the bond forged between my village and my school, two institutions that had shaped my journey in profound ways. That match, with all its absurdities and warmth, remains a cherished moment for those who took part—a celebration of tradition, camaraderie, and the enduring spirit of connection.

Whilst on the subject of sport, taking up golf in Port Moresby, in hindsight, was an act of brilliant foresight. Many of my schoolmates had turned into excellent golfers over the years, and those games became a chance to reconnect and reignite our old camaraderie. I vividly recall one memorable round at the Denarau resort golf course with my former school relay teammate Ratu Isoa Gavidi, and another old boy Keni Dakuidreketi (KD). On the final hole, a par 5, I struck the ball cleanly, watching with growing excitement as it slowly rolled into the hole—an eagle! Thrilled, I turned to Ratu Isoa and Keni, expecting shouts of admiration and animated congratulations. Instead, they were looking away pretending not to have seen the shot. Or perhaps both looked away, feigning utter indifference, as if my feat was as mundane as a practice swing.

Ah, old schoolmates—true to form, taking the piss out of each other, just as we had done back at QVS. It was the kind of teasing that only years of shared history could produce, rooted in affection and the unspoken bond of lifelong friendship.

Those days in Fiji felt almost idyllic, a harmonious blend of tradition, community, friendship, and family. They were moments to cherish, where the joy of shared laughter and connection left an indelible mark on our family.

Four and a half years passed in what felt like the blink of an eye before Shell called once again, this time with a promotion that would take us to a new city, Brisbane. While I was ready for the new challenge, I could not shake the feeling that my work in Fiji was not finished. The opportunity to help my country and contribute to Fijian Holdings had stirred something in me that would linger even as we prepared for this next chapter. In September 1992, with both excitement for what lay ahead and a deep reluctance to leave, we departed Fiji, carrying with us wonderful memories of one of the happiest chapters of our lives.

CHAPTER 25

BRISBANE—CHALLENGES, COMMUNITY, AND RESILIENCE

"Perfect one day, better the next"—the tourism slogan for Brisbane turned out to be remarkably close to the truth. For me, it was as ideal as it gets, a place where you could plan your day with nearly a 90% chance of uninterrupted blue skies. In this sunny, relaxed setting, it felt as though each day offered the chance for new beginnings. It was the perfect backdrop for a fresh chapter. A city of around one million people at the time, Brisbane was not as old or deeply rooted as Sydney or Melbourne, but it exuded a youthful energy and an unmistakeable sense of a city on the move. The Brisbane River, winding through the heart of the city, had its banks transformed into scenic promenades, riverside parks and natural mangrove walks that preserved local wildlife. In its warmth and vibrancy, Brisbane felt like a city poised on the edge of greatness—a place offering a constant invitation to embrace life's possibilities. The future seemed bright, and we felt a part of it from the start.

My new post as Operations Manager and Chairman's Representative for Shell in Queensland extended beyond mere operational oversight to include navigating the political and industry landscapes. Brisbane, with its bustling business community, demanded a deft touch in managing both corporate interests and local sensitivities. The role required adaptability and finesse, balancing a corporate presence with the unique challenges of a dynamic and growing city. My responsibilities soon expanded to encompass operations in New South Wales, and I was elected to the Confederation of Industries, Queensland's primary business lobbying group. Although working with politicians was not my favourite part of the job, I accepted it as a necessary aspect of my role.

We settled quickly into life in Brisbane. Lina began her educational journey, starting preschool then junior school with the wide-eyed curiosity of a child discovering the world, while Sarah embraced full-time motherhood and became an active member of the local Baha'i community. Lina also started violin lessons and, through her teacher, we adopted Mooshy, a moggy kitten who would become an integral part of our family for the next seventeen years. Brisbane seemed to wrap us in a feeling of comfort and belonging as our family life settled beautifully amid the city's sunny, welcoming atmosphere.

However, my professional life was soon marked by two significant incidents that tested my mettle. Unlike the earlier disaster I had faced in Fiji, these challenges thankfully did not result in any fatalities, but they left a lasting impression on me.

The first incident occurred shortly after we arrived. We were returning from a relaxing weekend on the Sunshine Coast when my car phone rang. It was a reporter asking for my comments on a fire raging at Shell's Brisbane oil terminal. Sarah often says she has only seen me change colour this drastically twice in forty years—one of those times was in that tense car ride back. If you are in the oil industry, responsible for operations, this is the kind of call you dread. As we approached Brisbane, a dense black plume of smoke loomed over the city, stark against the perfect blue sky. The scene before me felt like a gut punch. My immediate concerns were for any lives potentially endangered and the inevitable media scrutiny, but also with our contingency plans and its various scenarios, my mind steeped in urgency and responsibility.

Thankfully, the fire was confined to a single large storage tank, and our emergency team, along with the Brisbane Fire Department, quickly brought it under control. But the media storm was relentless—TV cameras, radio interviews and endless questions left little time for reflection and kept us in the public's eye. Both internal and government inquiries followed, ultimately attributing the fire to a spark from a faulty pump motor. By the end of the ordeal, I felt a bit older and considerably more seasoned in handling crises.

The second challenge came about due to a mix-up during an oil transfer from a nearby refinery. A shipment of gasoline was accidentally contaminated with diesel, resulting in the recall of thousands of litres delivered throughout Queensland and northern New South Wales. For three intense days, we worked around the clock, pumping contaminated fuel from customer tanks and transporting it back to the terminal. It was a high-stakes operation, where each decision felt like threading a needle under immense scrutiny. In the intensity and heavy scrutiny of the recall operation, there was a strange relief in discovering that it was diesel mixed into petrol rather than the reverse, as petrol in diesel engines could have led to catastrophic damage and danger to lives. It was one of those moments when you are genuinely grateful for small mercies.

Around this time, I was approached by the Fijian Ambassador to Australia to serve as Fiji's Honorary Consul for Queensland. I accepted the role with enthusiasm, as it allowed me to remain connected to Fiji and stay informed about the country's developments through regular discussions with visiting ministers. Beyond the diplomatic engagements, the role provided me with the opportunity to connect with Fijian immigrants and students in Brisbane, creating a community I would later reconnect with upon my return to Fiji. One of my proudest achievements was initiating a Fijian-language radio segment on a government-run station. It was like a gift to our people in diaspora—a way to keep the heartbeat of Fiji alive across miles of ocean—and I hoped it would continue to do so for years to come.

The honorary role complemented my duties as Chairman's Representative well, and having a diplomatic number plate and a special airport pass certainly streamlined some of my responsibilities. However, not all aspects of my role in Brisbane were as fulfilling.

One of the more challenging tasks I faced was streamlining operations and making certain posts redundant. It was a task I did not relish, especially when it involved friends and colleagues. I made every effort to soften the blow, using my industry contacts to help those affected secure new positions. The transitions were difficult but necessary, an inevitable part of adapting to the fast-paced changes in technology and organisational restructuring. One friend, Geoff Voller, comes to mind. Parting from Shell enabled him to change career and he went on to become a highly successful stockbroker.

Geoff often expressed his gratitude, insisting that the career change opened doors he never would have considered had he remained at Shell. It was a bittersweet reminder that, as you climb the ranks in any organisation, you must sometimes make tough decisions, especially in the face of rapid change.

After four and a half years in Brisbane, Shell once again recalled me to Melbourne, this time to take over as distribution manager for Shell Australia. And so, we prepared to move once more. However, my transfer was delayed when my intended replacement fell ill, leaving Shell scrambling to find an alternative candidate.

Fortunately, we had purchased a house in Melbourne's Caulfield North while still in Fiji, planning for our long-term future in Australia. It was as though a part of us had prepared for this chapter all along, waiting for the right moment to welcome us home. Initially, we had been posted to Brisbane instead, and the Caulfield house had patiently waited for us. This foresight proved invaluable when my transfer was delayed. As the new school term approached, Sarah, Lina and Mooshy settled directly into the Melbourne house and found a nearby school for Lina. After two months of untangling a series of internal organisational moves, a replacement was finally found, and I was free to head to Melbourne.

Brisbane had tested my resilience and adaptability, its challenges chiselling me into a sharper leader. As we prepared to leave, I took some moments to reflect on the friendships, the challenges and the small victories that had marked our time in this vibrant city. It was a chapter filled with lessons in leadership, resilience and the strength found in community—lessons that would serve me well as we moved forward into the next phase of our journey.

CHAPTER 26

A SPIRITUAL HOMECOMING AND SAYING GOODBYE TO SHELL

Our new home in Caulfield North felt like a true sanctuary. Centrally located, with a short tram ride to Lina's school, it brought a welcome sense of permanence. The garden, long neglected, became my weekend refuge—a place to untangle the week's challenges, let go of the week's pressures and find grounding in something simple. Lina adapted quickly to her new school, making friendships that would last for years, and Sera and Tracey, both in university, were moving forward with their lives. Mooshy, our spirited cat, had staked out her territory and was quick to enforce it. Melbourne was more than a base; as it was when I first moved here, it was a home with a feeling of continuity, a place we all felt ready to settle for the foreseeable future.

Back at Shell's Melbourne head office, however, the sense of stability was rapidly shifting. The company had embarked on a sweeping global restructuring, outsourcing various functions such as IT, engineering project management and engineering services to cut costs. Yet instead of moving these services to external firms, Shell established its own service companies, staffed by former Shell employees, who would now compete both for Shell projects and external contracts. In the ensuing changes, I was moved and promoted once more, taking up the role of the first CEO of Shell Engineering Services Ltd. for the Asia-Pacific region. My role was to manage this independent operation, transforming it from separate departments of various Shell companies in the region into a single self-sustaining business in a fiercely competitive field. This was to be my last promotion and my last job in Shell.

My new role spanned a vast and culturally diverse region: the Middle East through to Southeast Asia, Australia and New Zealand. It did not include Saudi Arabia, China and Japan, but still, with a territory that vast, the challenge for me was to bridge geographic and cultural divides while transforming Shell Engineering Services into a lean, competitive entity—a feat that demanded resilience and innovation. I found the biggest and the most challenging task of all, however, lay in changing the mindset of Shell employees, for whom guaranteed projects and security had become familiar foundations. Now, we had to compete for Shell projects and secure outside contracts to turn a profit, working with a new sense of independence and urgency. It was a challenging task but invigorating—a new frontier that gave me renewed energy as demands for our service grew.

Meanwhile, an inner transformation was also taking place. Over the years, Sarah's unwavering devotion to the Baha'i Faith ignited a quiet questioning within me—a search for values that transcended corporate success and could bridge the moral divides I observed in the world. I was raised in a traditionally Christian family, and my Fijian background brought with it a strong sense of spirituality. Yet, I was finding myself increasingly troubled by what I saw as a lack of integrity and genuine ethics in both private and public sectors across the world. There was a deep-seated issue: a corrosion of trust and a tolerance for corruption that seemed to affect both systems. Without a balanced approach—a blending of spiritual values with practical action—neither the private sector nor government could fully serve the people. It would be akin to a bird with one damaged wing—it needs both wings to soar.

The Baha'i teachings spoke directly to these dilemmas, addressing both spiritual growth and the ways it could influence practical aspects of life. I also always found a sense of alignment in the Baha'i principle to "let deeds, not words, be your adorning," which, amongst other teachings, resonated with my personal philosophy. Could one person's actions—through honest behaviour, transparency and adherence to principles—make a difference? For a long time, I had been acting in accordance with these values but without formally embracing the Baha'i Faith. Still, I hesitated, caught between my traditional loyalty to family beliefs and my growing conviction in a worldview that offered hope, balance and practicality.

Then, one morning in 2001, just before Lina's twelfth birthday, I was heading downstairs when she looked up at me from the bottom of the stairs with a question I had not expected: "Daddy, why aren't you a Baha'i?" Lina's innocent yet profound question shattered the walls of indecision I had built around myself. In her unfiltered wisdom, she illuminated a path I had long been circling but had not yet dared to take. I knew right then that I was ready. It felt strangely inevitable, as though this moment had simply been waiting for me. Wanting to surprise her, I said something innocuous as an answer then went through the declaration process quietly. My Baha'i membership card arrived just in time for her birthday, and I tucked it in with her gifts. When she opened it, Lina let out a delighted shriek, running to give me a huge hug. In that moment, I felt an overwhelming peace—a feeling that I had truly come home. This feeling was cemented when as a family we visited the Baha'i World Centre in Haifa, Israel, late in the same year.

At Shell, the task of forging a new identity for Shell Engineering Services was in full swing. I put every employee through a 'Focus' workshop, which I modelled on Al Reis' book of the same name, to accelerate the changes I needed to do. Stripping away years of Shell's protective corporate culture was not easy, and we faced setbacks along the way, including the loss of a few Shell contracts. But gradually, through total focus on the way forward, a new awareness of our independence grew among the team, sparking a competitive spirit. It forged a new spirit of resilience and innovation within the team, culminating in the hard-earned success of becoming one of Shell's first profitable service companies.

Despite our success, it was becoming increasingly clear that Melbourne was not the right base for Shell Engineering Services. Our largest operations were based in Singapore, near the major Asia-Pacific refinery, and relocating there made practical sense. But the thought of yet another move, especially with Lina thriving in her Melbourne school, was difficult for Sarah and me. We both felt we had already uprooted our family enough.

Sensing that Shell's transformation might be marking the natural end of my journey with them, I took the matter up directly with Ian Freer, Shell's Group Coordinator for Services, and Peter Duncan, Shell Australia's Chairman. They asked the inevitable question: "What would you like to do?" I gave a frank answer. I wanted to go home to Fiji to put the experience I had gained to meaningful use. I felt the time had come to give something back in the only area I knew well—the corporate sector. Both Ian and Peter understood, and soon we reached an agreement. I would go to Fiji to gauge the need and, if the opportunity existed, Shell would allow me to step down with a financial package. I would also serve as Chairman of Shell Fiji for the next three years, remaining connected to Shell in a way that felt purpose driven.

After discussing the decision with Sarah, we agreed it was the right move. Sarah, ever supportive, had only one condition: I would return to Melbourne once a month, and she and Lina would join me in Fiji during school holidays. It was a balance we could work with, and soon I was on a plane back to Fiji to meet with Prime Minister Qarase and the Energy Minister. They welcomed my offer, and I returned to Melbourne with an invitation to chair the state-owned Fiji Electricity Authority, helping guide it through the upcoming deregulation.

Leaving Shell in 2001 was bittersweet. I had grown with Shell, and Shell had given me a career, personal growth, the fulfilment of a long-held dream and a sense of purpose that transcended the professional world. Saying goodbye to friends and colleagues—many of whom had become like family—was profoundly emotional. But walking out of Shell's doors for the final time, I carried with me a profound sense of gratitude for a journey that had enriched my life immeasurably, coupled with a deep anticipation for the uncharted roads awaiting me in Fiji. Looking ahead, I felt the pull of a new purpose, and I knew that this next chapter promised rewards that perhaps even Shell could not have prepared me for.

CHAPTER 27

A NEW CHAPTER OF PURPOSE

When I stepped away from Shell, I was not merely closing a door but opening one with a higher calling. Here was my chance to make a difference for Fiji—not for my own profit or ambition, but for the people of my country. I could not only contribute but also challenge entrenched systems and to mould a corporate culture to one rooted in integrity and purpose. In May 2001, I returned to my roots as Chairman of the FEA, a monopoly and my first employer. Coming full circle, I was back, now with a clear mandate to enact long-overdue changes. I carried with me a wealth of experience, a newfound clarity of purpose, and a readiness to challenge the status quo.

The FEA was under pressure to deregulate, and I quickly recognised the deep cultural shifts required to help it survive in a competitive environment. What I had not anticipated was just how entrenched its issues were. FEA, steeped in titles and hierarchy, was also shackled by antiquated practices, a culture of entitlement and a glaring disconnect between leadership and operational effectiveness—barriers I was determined to dismantle. Every manager had to have a grand office and a secretary—not one could send an email themselves; handwritten notes were still being typed out by secretaries and sent as official communications through emails.

Reports commissioned at great expense sat untouched, while the board merely rubber-stamped decisions without scrutiny. The culture of entitlement was pervasive. The staggering disconnect between leadership and operational efficacy had eroded not only public trust but the sense of accountability within the organisation.

One telling incident occurred when I was still with Shell. A colleague rang me, mentioning how he had met a Fijian executive at a conference. However, after registering on the first day, the executive disappeared entirely from the event. At the time, I dismissed it as inconsequential. But, after taking over as Chairman of FEA, I discovered the executive held a senior position at FEA. Upon reviewing contracts, I unearthed a disturbing trend: senior managers had entitlements for two overseas 'conference' trips of their choice annually with no requirement to account for them afterwards. It became glaringly clear that these trips were being exploited as opportunities for private leisure under the guise of professional development.

This discovery only strengthened my resolve. The depth of complacency, entitlement and unaccountability was astonishing. It was apparent that immediate, transformational changes were required, starting with the removal of those who exploited the system. I also realised that to truly drive reform, I needed broader authority. Securing the role of Executive Chairman gave me the latitude to drive sweeping reforms—eliminating privileges masked as entitlements and cultivating a culture of accountability that began to ripple through the organisation.

With this newfound authority, I set about restructuring FEA's leadership. The first order of business was finding a CEO aligned with my vision of integrity-driven management. I found that in a young, dynamic engineer named Rokoseru Nabalarua from the private sector. Ethical, capable and unafraid of confronting tough changes, he embodied the principles I sought to instil within the organisation. His natural leadership and commitment to transparency brought a breath of fresh air to the FEA.

From the outset, my goal was clear: to reshape FEA around ethical leadership. It was to be guided by principles and grounded in purpose as I had done with Shell Service Engineering. I formed a Change Management team that reported directly to me, and together we tackled the deep-seated issues that had long been ignored. We disciplined anyone involved in malfeasance, streamlined management titles and dismantled the entitlement culture by eliminating unnecessary perks such as these extravagant jaunts thinly disguised as so-called conference trips. Managers were encouraged to adopt hands-on roles and modernise their practices. The results were palpable—customer satisfaction improved, employee morale lifted and FEA's public image began to shift. FEA's transformation, while gradual, began to inspire confidence among employees and the public alike.

But our early success came with an unexpected consequence: unwanted media attention. The press, particularly vocal about public institutions, seized on FEA's turnaround. Almost overnight, I found myself in the headlines—an unusual and uncomfortable change for someone accustomed to working behind the scenes. While it was gratifying to see FEA's improvements recognised, the media attention brought a level of scrutiny and visibility that came with its own set of challenges. The sense of anonymity I once valued faded, replaced by a high-profile persona that inadvertently set me up as a target. Although I had not yet grasped the full significance, this exposure was planting seeds for what would later become a liability in a nation as politically sensitive as Fiji.

The government, meanwhile, pleased with the transformation at FEA, soon tasked me with replicating this success across other state-owned enterprises. My next assignment was to lead Telecom Fiji Ltd. (TFL) through deregulation, a process that had already opened the door to international competitors like Vodafone. The challenge was significant: to modernise the organization while competing against nimble global players who thrived on innovation and efficiency. It was a daunting task, but one I approached with the same sense of purpose and resolve that had guided my work at FEA.

The fundamental issues at TFL were similar to those I had faced at FEA, but they were exacerbated by the fact that some competitors were already being established and by the organisation's entrenched state monopoly attitudes and practices. The top management, led by an ex-civil servant, was entirely out of its depth in competing with the agile and resourceful private sector entrants. It was clear that the existing leadership structure lacked the vision and expertise necessary to navigate this new and highly competitive landscape.

Recognizing the urgency of the situation, I temporarily took over as Managing Director, implementing a 'shock and awe' approach to change management, much as I had done at FEA. I also brought in a new Chief Financial Officer and a new Marketing Manager from the private sector—a move that injected much-needed dynamism and professionalism into the organization.

The message was clear: complacency was no longer an option.

The transformation was swift. Within months, TFL began to shed its outdated practices, reconnecting with customer needs and embracing the demands of a fast-moving telecommunications landscape. The shift in culture and operations was palpable. TFL was no longer a relic of a bygone era but a competitor with renewed purpose and resilience, proving that even the most entrenched institutions could adapt and thrive with a new vision and renewed sense of purpose and urgency driven by a focused leadership.

As my work continued, the government called on me to support other national initiatives. I joined Fijian Holdings Ltd. (FHL) as Deputy Chairman and later had the privilege of serving as Chairman of an organization particularly dear to me—an entity I had helped establish in the 1980s to foster indigenous Fijian participation in business. This role felt like a full-circle moment, reconnecting me with an initiative that had always been close to my heart.

My involvement with FHL led to another remarkable chapter. In 2001, FHL acquired the internationally renowned Blue Lagoon Cruises from its owner, David Wilson. By 2002, I had become Chairman of Blue Lagoon Cruises, a position I held until the coup of 2006 forced significant changes. Though the circumstances that ended my tenure were tumultuous, my connection to the company remained a meaningful part of my professional journey.

Years later, in 2010, after settling in Cheltenham, UK, Sarah and I began adjusting to our new surroundings. During this period, Sarah reconnected with an old friend from her postgraduate MBA class (1975–1977) at the London Business School, John Kennedy and his wife Ann. Now retired and living in Bristol, John and Ann joined us for lunch at our home. It was a pleasant reunion, marked by shared memories and lively conversation.

Then, as we chatted, life delivered one of its astonishing twists. John and Ann revealed that not only were they close friends of the Wilsons, but John had also been a director of Blue Lagoon Cruises before its acquisition by Fijian Holdings. Suddenly, across continents and decades, our lives converged in the most unexpected way. Here we were, sitting around a table in Cheltenham, discovering a shared connection to a company that had played a not-insignificant role in both our lives.

It was a moment that left me marvelling at the inexplicable serendipity of life. How unlikely it seemed that, half a world away, I would meet an ex-fellow director of a company I had once chaired—someone who also shared a bond with my wife from her postgraduate days forty years ago. Such are the unpredictable threads of life, weaving connections that defy logic yet leave an indelible impression.

Soon, I was tasked with setting up additional government entities, including the Fiji Audio Visual Commission, the Fiji Investment Trust (the nation's sovereign fund), the Fiji Fiscal Review Committee and I joined the Prime minister's think tank group to advise him on many issues that confronted Fiji then and into the future. Each role was an opportunity to apply principles of ethical governance and to give back meaningfully to Fiji's corporate sector. Through these roles, I was given a unique vantage point, but once again the media was keenly interested in these long-overdue transformations.

The spotlight, once focused on the FEA, now tracked every change and decision across these initiatives, further amplifying my visibility.

To nurture the next generation of indigenous Fijian leaders, I assembled a cohort of promising young Fijian executives, fostering a dialogue on ethical leadership and embedding the values of transparency and service into the DNA of our future leaders. Among them were Rokoseru and others who would later take on significant leadership roles in both public and private sectors. These gatherings allowed us to explore the ethical underpinnings of leadership, reinforcing the foundations of transparency that I hoped would permeate Fiji's future corporate culture. As Mr Kamikamica was my role model, I tried to be also a role model for these future leaders.

However, while I was immersed in these efforts, political tensions simmered beneath the surface. As a member of the Baha'i Faith, I had always maintained a strictly apolitical stance, focusing solely on service and ethical leadership. But my increasing visibility in transforming public institutions brought unintended risks. Inadvertently, it placed me at the nexus of corporate reform and political sensitivity, a place I never intended to be and a precarious position in Fiji's fragile landscape.

CHAPTER 28

THE COUP AND THE
UNCERTAIN ROAD AHEAD

On 5 December 2006, the nation was shocked when the Commander of the Fiji Military Forces, Bainimarama, staged a coup, seizing control of the government.

The news came abruptly while I was on holiday in Melbourne with my family. One afternoon, the phone rang; it was a journalist from the Fiji media asking for my reaction to the coup that had just occurred. "What coup?" I asked, taken aback. That was when I learned that Bainimarama was now in control and had delivered a public blow by announcing my removal from all state boards—a swift dismantling of the progress and trust I had worked so tirelessly to build. The suddenness of it all left me stunned. All the work, energy, passion and vision I had poured into transforming Fiji's institutions seemed to be undone in an instant. My immediate thoughts turned to the ordinary people and the businesses of Fiji who would now face the consequences of yet another coup—the fourth since 1987.

As this was happening, I reflected on the work we had accomplished and the hope that the nascent reforms had sprouted some roots. Despite the turbulent political landscape, I felt a deep sense of fulfilment knowing

I had tried to make a tangible difference, but I could not quell my lingering questions—would the seeds of change we had sown endure or wither amid the turbulence of political unrest? Was I even prepared to navigate the treacherous waters that lay ahead under this new regime?

I never imagined that the journey I had taken to serve Fiji would end this way. When I left Shell, it was with the hope of making a meaningful difference in my homeland. Yet, as I looked out on the years of work that now seemed to be at a crossroad between crumbling or continuing, I found myself asking if any of it had truly mattered. Had it been enough? Had I been naïve to believe that change was possible? Was I prepared to work under this new illegal regime? I did not think I would but, as it turned out, the decision was made for me.

As the news sank in, it became clear that the attention I had received in the media for my efforts to reform state enterprises had likely painted a target on my back. Bainimarama, quietly observing from the sidelines, must have identified people he saw as threats to his power. In his eyes, my public profile—built around transforming entities like the FEA—had grown too prominent. The irony was stark: the very visibility that had once supported my work was now a liability. I was now paying the price for trying to make things better, for being too visible, too influential.

Determined to resolve the situation, I flew back to Fiji with one goal in mind: to set the record straight. I had no political ambitions—being a Baha'i, it was impossible for me to even consider entering the political arena. My sole intention was to elevate the institutions of Fiji, to groom young leaders and to serve the country with integrity. But for reasons I could not fully understand, Bainimarama refused to meet with me. Undeterred, I insisted that my message be passed through the appropriate channels. I wanted it to be clear that I harboured no ambitions beyond my work and that my intentions were as they had always been—to serve my country honestly. In a country where the smallest misstep could lead to imprisonment, it was crucial to ensure he understood my intentions. Whether it was this message or pure luck that spared me from the fate of so many others, I will never know. Unlike several of my colleagues who were detained on questionable charges, I was left alone, but the uncertainty was ever-present.

In the days following the coup, Bainimarama's true agenda began to take shape. To pacify international governments and organisations, he issued vague promises of holding elections "in due course" after ridding the country of so-called "bad elements." The world, eager to avoid conflict, seemed all too willing to take him at his word. For many Fijians, the disillusionment was immediate, but we knew that in the international arena, promises often trumped actions, at least in the short term.

Behind this diplomatic facade, a darker plan was unfolding. Bainimarama appeared to be systematically eliminating potential rivals. He began by getting rid of key public officers, including the Chief Justice, and replacing them with appointees who were expected to be loyal to his regime. A so-called anti-corruption agency— the Fiji Independent Commission Against Corruption (FICAC)—was established and quickly went to work targeting perceived opponents, including the elected Prime Minister. These individuals were prosecuted on questionable charges, ensuring that a compliant judiciary would convict them and disqualify them from political activity. Meanwhile, travel bans were issued under the pretence of ongoing investigations, trapping influential figures within Fiji's borders and effectively silencing them. Within three years, the legal checks and balances that support democracy and the rule of law—built over decades—had been dismantled one element at a time, leaving a compliant and controlled apparatus in their place.

It was during this tumultuous time that I received another shock. After returning from Britain, where Sarah and I had gone to arrange her mother's funeral, I discovered that my own name had been added to the travel ban list. I could no longer leave Fiji. The discovery was chilling—a stark reminder of how tenuous personal freedoms had become under a regime that brooked no dissent. I had done nothing wrong, and my conscience was clear. But with all the institutions of power under Bainimarama's control, the fear of being falsely accused and imprisoned was ever-present. Every day felt like a gamble, as if a roll of the dice would determine who would be next to be arrested. Life had become an unpredictable blend of tension and resignation, with even the simplest routines clouded by a shadow of uncertainty.

Amidst the escalating tension, I felt a deep yearning to return to my village of Naroi. So, that Christmas, I gathered my three daughters, my siblings and their families for what felt like a final pilgrimage. The village welcomed us with open arms and, for a few precious weeks, we found solace in the simplicity of village life. Away from the stress and political turmoil of Suva, I felt a sense of peace, a reconnection with my roots. It was the tonic I needed, and our stay was memorable, filled with laughter, warmth and moments of sheer hilarity.

I will never forget the 'capture' of my youngest daughter Lina, and three of her cousins on New Year's morning. It was during the village custom of *qiri kapa* when, at the stroke of midnight, groups of young people would march around in raucous steel bands, banging on old metal containers and producing an extraordinary cacophony of sound. The processions would compete to see which group could be the loudest, and the village echoed with laughter as water was thrown on them from all directions—each splash greeted with cheer and good humour.

A lesser-known tradition, however, added an unexpected twist to the festivities. If a young maiden was found at another clan's house by sunrise, she would be considered 'captured' and unable to leave until her family presented a *tabua* (whale's tooth – a highly regarded traditional gift) for her release. Lina and her cousins, blissfully unaware of this custom, had accepted an 'innocent' invitation for tea at dawn from another clan. By sunrise, their fate was sealed—they had been officially 'captured.'

Their fathers—my brothers George and Tevita and I— still recovering from a heavy night of kava drinking, were unceremoniously roused to negotiate their release. Bleary-eyed and slightly amused, we scrambled to assemble the traditional gifts required for their freedom. It turned into a costly yet uproarious episode, the laughter and ribbing echoing long after the cousins were safely back with us.

The hilarity of that morning underscored the spirit of the village—deeply rooted in tradition yet brimming with humour and joy. And yet, beneath the peace and laughter of that pilgrimage was a quiet sadness—a realisation that I might never return. Each familiar sight and sound held a bittersweet quality, as if I were gathering memories to carry with me into an uncertain future.

Returning to Suva was like stepping back into a cauldron of uncertainty. The stress was palpable and the fear of what might happen next was suffocating. Sarah, still grieving her mother's death, came back to Fiji to stand by my side. Together, we navigated this turbulent period. It was painful to watch as the work I had dedicated myself to was dismantled by self-serving individuals loyal to the new regime. Had all my efforts been for nothing? Had my years of service, driven by a deep commitment to uplift the people, simply been discarded?

In the aftermath of the coup, I also faced a profound test of moral integrity and loyalty when the elected Prime Minister was arrested. His defence team reached out to friends and colleagues, including me, asking us to testify on his behalf. After consulting with Sarah and my brother George, we unanimously agreed on one guiding principle: to do what was just and right, regardless of the consequences. In the end, I stood as the only witness for the Prime Minister—a sobering reflection on the fragility of friendships forged in the crucible of politics. Many, fearing for their own safety, chose to stay silent, while others, perhaps more grievously, colluded with the regime to secure their positions. It was a stark reminder of the high cost of standing for truth in a time of betrayal.

To this day, I am deeply disturbed by the disgraceful treatment meted out to the elected Prime Minister. He was relentlessly persecuted and hounded in ways that were both unfair and undeserved. The actions perpetrated by Bainimarama and his supporters were personal, petty and vindictive, revealing a level of spitefulness that transcended any sense of justice or governance. In my view, any punishment Bainimarama and his accomplices face through proper and due process of law would not only be justified but, at the very least, well deserved.

Yet, in those darkest moments of political turmoil and personal uncertainty, the teachings of the Baha'i Faith became both my anchor and my unswerving compass, reminding me that justice and service endure even in the shadow of oppression. I found strength in a prayer revealed by the Báb:

> *"Is there any Remover of difficulties save God? Say: Praised be God! He is God! All are His servants, and all abide by His bidding."*

The phrase "All abide by His bidding" reminded me that, even in chaos, there could be a higher purpose at work. It was not for me to question why these things were happening, but to trust that, ultimately, good would prevail. Another piece from the Baha'i writings, 'The Hidden Words', offered me comfort:

> *"O oppressors on earth! Withdraw your hands from tyranny, for I have pledged Myself not to forgive any man's injustice."*

Each line was a steady reminder that no act of service, however disregarded by others, was in vain. I realised I was part of a journey far greater than one career or one set of ambitions. These words were a balm to my spirit, reminding me that the arc of justice, though slow, ultimately bends towards what is right.

Then, one evening, as the golden light of dusk bathed the quiet streets of Suva, the phone rang. The voice on the other end was familiar—it was the Director of Immigration. "Joe," he said, "I'm sitting in front of my computer, and I am removing your name from the travel ban as we speak."

The relief was immediate, like a heavy weight lifted from my shoulders. I turned to Sarah and told her to book two return tickets to Melbourne on the first available flight. We would pack light—just a suitcase each—and, to craft a facade of normalcy, we booked return tickets, masking our departure as a temporary visit—a calculated move to outmanoeuvre the ever-watchful regime.

On the morning of February 13, 2008, over a year after the coup, we boarded a flight from Nadi International Airport to Melbourne. As the plane ascended into the sky, I looked out the window at the receding island below. Fiji had given me so much—my upbringing, my purpose, my drive to serve. But now, it was time to say goodbye. Whether I would ever return was uncertain, but I knew that, for now, it was the end of a chapter. There was a mix of sorrow and acceptance and a sense that life was leading me to a place I had not foreseen but one I was finally ready for.

As I gazed into the horizon, leaving the island behind, I carried with me the hope that the seeds I had planted would one day bear fruit. The story was not over—not for Fiji, and certainly not for me. Perhaps, in ways I could not yet see, Fiji's journey and mine were forever entwined, each sustaining the other in its own way.

Bainimarama ruled as an unopposed tyrant for eight years. He systematically dismantled political opposition, imprisoning potential rivals on trumped-up charges and ensuring that all government institutions were headed by loyal supporters. After consolidating his power, he formed his own political party and called an election in 2014, securing a resounding but dubious victory, as expected. He repeated his win in the 2018 election. Though officially the head of two successive civilian governments, his governance bore the hallmarks of authoritarianism, bolstered by his large parliamentary majorities. But overconfidence bred complacency, and in the 2022 election, he was defeated by a coalition of three political parties—losing by a slim margin of just three votes.

As I write this memoir in 2024, I reflect on the unfolding of events with a renewed sense of clarity. Bainimarama and some of his key accomplices have now faced the weight of justice, charged and imprisoned under the due process of Fiji's laws. Even more serious charges loom on the horizon, a testament to the inevitability of accountability. It seems, as I once wrote, that "the arc of justice, though slow, ultimately bends towards what is right."

This moment is not just a vindication of principles but a reassurance to all who have ever faced injustice— that truth, though often delayed, will eventually emerge. The wheels of justice may grind slowly, but they do grind, aligning with the divine assurance that no act of tyranny goes unaddressed. For Fiji, this marks a step towards healing and redemption, a reaffirmation that no matter how deep the darkness, the light of justice will find its way.

And so, with each passing year, I continue to hold faith in the profound truth that what is right will ultimately prevail. If such an outcome can arise in a small and often overlooked corner of the world like Fiji, it offers hope for the rest of humanity, irrespective of the size of the nation or the scale of the injustice, the principles of fairness and accountability have the power to transcend borders and inspire change.

CHAPTER 29

RENEWAL AND NEW BEGINNINGS

Back in Melbourne, the absence of a clear purpose left me with an unsettling sense of emptiness. After so many years of purposeful, high-stakes work, the stillness of retirement felt both alien and hollow—a stark contrast to the purpose-driven life I had left behind. Yet having Sera and Tracey nearby brought a welcome comfort. Both had finished their university studies and were forging their own respective careers. We saw each other regularly, catching up on their lives and sharing precious moments in person rather than through hurried phone calls. Lina was turning out to be an adventurous young lady taking up extreme hiking as a hobby which often unsettled her mother. I also found solace in the Baha'i activities, though not with the same deep involvement as Sarah. We travelled a bit, including a visit to Lina in Paris, where she was spending her year of service with the Baha'i community. But overall, the pace of retirement was a far cry from the demanding life I had known before.

Two wonderful events marked this quieter chapter of our lives. On 10 December 2009, Tracey and her partner Nick welcomed their first child, my granddaughter, Nisi. Her arrival infused our lives with new light, her name a tender tribute to my mother and a bridge between the generations—a continuation of love that connected past to present and a way of keeping her Fijian heritage alive. Then, on February 27, 2010, Sera married her partner, Ben Teniswood. Watching them exchange vows, I could not help but feel a wave of nostalgia. I saw them again as young girls, laughing and running through the streets of Lautoka, their small hands gripping mine as they splashed around on the beaches of Natadola, the ocean and the endless horizons before them. They had grown into strong, independent women, building their own families. It was a poignant reminder of life's full circle.

While Melbourne offered comfort, it was clear that Sarah was yearning for a return to her roots. The call to return to Cheltenham, the town where she grew up, became stronger, especially after the passing of her mother. Her brother, Charles, diagnosed with Asperger's syndrome, needed support, though sadly he passed away within six months of our arrival. By May 2010, we made what we hoped would be our final move—to the UK—leaving Lina behind to finish her degree at Monash University.

Lina joined us a year later after completing her studies and taking up an internship with Lush Ltd., which soon turned into a full-time job in Poole, where Lush's headquarter is. She later joined the BBC in London, where she now lives. From our humble beginnings in the village of Naroi, our family had now spread across the globe— from Fiji to Australia, and now to the UK. It was as if our family's journey, which began with simple roots, had expanded to touch distant shores, a reality that would have seemed unimaginable to my mother. I believed my father would have smiled at the journey's reach.

We brought Mooshy, our beloved cat from Brisbane, with us. Pets, particularly cats, have a unique way of becoming an inseparable part of the family. They not only bring joy but also often mirror our own eccentricities. Mooshy was no different. She came with her quirks and an independent spirit, making her a source of endless amusement and comfort. The lengths we went to accommodate her—from expensive vet bills to airfares higher than our own—were proof enough that we had become true pet lovers.

Mooshy had a way of making her presence felt, particularly during our Baha'i devotional gatherings. Whenever a Persian friend chanted prayers, Mooshy would meow along, trying to harmonise in her own feline way. Lina's friends from school also had amusing tales (and a few scratches) to remember her by, as Mooshy only tolerated Lina's affectionate strokes. These antics always brought laughter and life to our home. The grand spectacle, however, was her showdown with the neighbour's cats soon after we moved into our new home in Cheltenham.

On one unforgettable night, we were woken up by the bloodcurdling sounds of a catfight echoing through the house. Rushing downstairs, we found Mooshy in the kitchen, her back arched and fur fluffed up like porcupine quills. Tufts of black cat hair covered the floor as she hissed victoriously, seemingly declaring to any intruders, "My house, my people, stay out!" After that dramatic night, no neighbour's cat dared to cross our threshold again. It was the first time we felt fully claimed by the house, with Mooshy as our fearless guardian. The final confirmation that we had truly found our new home in this country came when we picked up Mooshy from Heathrow's pet lounge—far more luxurious than the human airport waiting areas. It made us smile that we were amongst a nation of fellow cat lovers!

Finding coincidences in life is something of a marvel. The way life seemed to weave together such improbable events sometimes left me in awe. One of the first things I did when we arrived in Cheltenham was to try and find out if there were any Fijians living in town. A glance through the phonebook yielded nothing, but I decided to try the local rugby club next. While Cheltenham was not a rugby league town, I knew a few Fijians had been recruited to play in the UK and thought there might be a chance. To my surprise, the club did have one Fijian associated with it—a masseur named Mala—but he was away on holiday. In Fijian, Mala is like Jim—a shortened version of something else. I knew a few Malas, just as I would a few Jims. They gave me a phone number, and I left the club, curious who this Mala might be.

I decided to call the number. An English lady answered, which tempered my hopes. I explained the reason for my call and, to my surprise, she confirmed that she was married to a Fijian man named Mala. Intrigued, I asked for his full name, and she replied "Malamalanitabua." I did not know of anyone by that name, but I pressed on, asking which school he had attended in Fiji. When she said QVS, my pulse quickened. Could he be the same Malamala I had known all those years ago? I ventured to ask, "Would he have been called Malamala at school?" She laughed, confirming, "The one and only. He used the shortened version of his name at school." Astonished, I realised I had stumbled upon a long-lost schoolmate from my days at QVS—someone I had not seen in over

45 years. To cross paths in this English town was a coincidence so remarkable it felt almost destined. We immediately set a date for a reunion dinner, and it was indeed wonderful and heart-warming to catch up and exchange our respective journeys' stories and to introduce our respective spouses.

But life was not done surprising me. A few years later, Mala's wife, Ann, sadly passed away, prompting him to return to Fiji for an extended visit. While there, he married another woman and eventually brought her back to England. To my utter astonishment, his new wife turned out to be Donita Simmons—the very same Donita I had mentioned earlier in this book, my classmate from the Higher Education Course at Suva Grammar School. The odds of such a reconnection already felt extraordinary, but the story did not end there.

A few weeks later, as we continued our habit of seeking out fellow Fijians in the area, Mala and Donita mentioned meeting a young Fijian couple living in Brockworth, a small village just eight miles away. The couple, Alex and Mere Swan, had been recruited into the British Army in Fiji and, after completing their service, they had settled in the UK. Eager to connect with them, we naturally invited them over for dinner, along with Mala and Donita. When Alex and Mere arrived at our home, the coincidences deepened yet again—Mere turned out to be the granddaughter of my first cousin from our village in Fiji! In the span of weeks, Cheltenham had gone from feeling like a quiet corner of England to becoming a small hub of unexpected Fijian connections, with three families now intertwined in the most serendipitous of ways.

These coincidences, though perhaps small in the grand scheme of life, brought immeasurable richness to this chapter of my journey. It is moments like these that underscore the profound interconnectedness of human existence across time and distance, creating bonds that seem predestined in their unfolding and, for that, I remain deeply grateful.

Finding our new home in Cheltenham was a process of its own. We were looking for a place that would accommodate not just our family life but also our future Baha'i gatherings and devotions. The moment we stepped into the house that would eventually become ours, we knew it was the one. The house seemed to speak to us with a quiet promise—a space ready to nurture both family life and the gatherings that would soon breathe warmth and purpose into its walls. The garden was a neglected canvas, ready for transformation, while the house itself had a kitchen that Sarah envisioned turning into a hub for entertaining. Fourteen years later, as I write this, that first instinct has proven true.

What followed was a whirlwind of renovations and transformations. All the pent-up energy from the stressful years in Fiji found an outlet as I took on project management once again—this time for our home. Inside, we merged bedrooms to create an ensuite, redesigned the kitchen into an open-plan living space and added a conservatory. Meanwhile, outside, landscapers worked on the garden to my design, planting over 330 plants, many of which were English roses. The garden became my sanctuary, a place where I could reconnect with the cycles of nature.

Winter, however, brought its own challenges. The coldest and snowiest Cheltenham had seen since 1962, it turned our renovation site into a quagmire. Contractors jostled for parking space, blocking footpaths and drawing the attention of friendly police community support officers. We cooked on camping stoves in a makeshift kitchen as snow turned to slush. Despite the chaos, it was exhilarating. The house, the garden and even the mess reminded me that I was alive and thriving once again. As I watched the snow blanket our street, I felt for the first time the serene beauty of winter—a peaceful contrast to the fast-paced urgency that had once filled my days. It showed me another side to nature's tapestry of seasonal beauty and the peaceful sound of silence that accompanied it.

By the following spring, our garden came to life. Watching the roses bloom and the plants flourish was like witnessing a miracle. For the first time in years, I allowed myself the simple pleasure of 'smelling the roses.' We opened our garden to friends and neighbours as part of charity events for the British Red Cross, raising funds for global disasters. These gatherings became joyful affairs, complete with cream teas prepared by Sarah and Fijian sing-alongs led by recently retired Fijian servicemen and women in the area. These gatherings felt like a new form of service, one woven with community and culture, where our past met our present. It was our way of continuing the spirit of service we had cultivated in Fiji in our adopted home.

The house also became a gathering place for the local Baha'i community, and life in the UK began to find its own rhythm. The garden blossomed, friendships deepened and, gradually, we began to feel truly at home. Among the friendships that enriched this chapter of our lives were Paul and Clare Hemelryk, whose warm hospitality and genuine welcome made our transition to Cheltenham seamless.

Clare, with her remarkable talent for mimicry and razor-sharp puns that could rival any professional comedian, infused every gathering with vibrant humour and infectious energy. Her husband, Paul, a solicitor with a dry wit and a calm, sagacious demeanour, became not only a trusted advisor during our property search and purchase but also a trusted influence in our lives. Ever the voice of reason, Paul had a unique ability to keep both our self-proclaimed "brilliant" spouses grounded—a task that required no small amount of skill and patience! Their shared sense of humour, so cleverly intertwined with their wisdom and generosity, has been an endless source of joy, and their friendship a true treasure.

This chapter of our lives, which began amid the turbulence of a coup, had brought us to a place of tranquillity, community, deep friendship and renewed purpose. Friends like Paul and Clare were more than companions on this journey; they were part of the vibrant fabric that made Cheltenham feel like home.

Amidst the joy, however, came moments of profound personal loss. While we had already lost two of my siblings, Kata and Jone in earlier years, and Cakacaka and Sarah's brother Charles earlier on our arrival in England, the period between December 2021 and August 2024 presented us an unexpected cascade of farewells. My four remaining siblings—George (December 2021), Sera (November 2023), Sisi (March 2024) and Tevita (August 2024)—also passed away. The unrelenting loss of all my remaining siblings left an ache that felt immeasurable, yet it was my beloved Tracey's passing in 2017 that shattered the core of my being—a grief unmatched and unending. The untimeliness of her passing, at the height of her life, tested my resilience in ways I could never have imagined. That loss remains the deepest wound of all, a profound sorrow that defies words and yet reminds me of the fragility and beauty of life itself.

But there were also moments of joy to balance the sorrow. On 3 December 2014, Sera and Ben welcomed a baby boy, Monty and, because we share a middle name: Banivanua, I affectionately call him Yaca (Fijian for 'name's sake')—a common practice in Fijian culture. The arrival of Monty felt like a ray of sunshine breaking through the clouds—a symbol of life's continuity in its simplest and most beautiful form. As I watched this new generation carrying forward our family's spirit, I was reminded of the enduring legacy of love and connection that binds us all and this fragile life that continues to bloom in unexpected ways.

CHAPTER 30

TRACEY—A JOURNEY OF LOVE,
LOSS, AND FAITH

Tracey's fierce independence, embodied in her childhood declaration "I can by myself" defined her life—a blend of determined resilience, boundless love and intellectual vigour that left an indelible mark on all who knew her. She and Nick had their second child, Jimmy, on 17 May 2013. By then, Tracey had risen to the rank of Associate Professor at La Trobe University in Melbourne. Her life seemed rich—balancing motherhood, a burgeoning academic career and a life filled with purpose. When she and Nick visited us in the UK, with young Nisi in tow, it was clear how deeply she had settled into her life, embracing both her roles as a mother and a scholar. Her joy radiated through her every word, her laughter infectious. We cherished every moment of their time with us in Cheltenham.

Yet, life is as mysterious as it is cruel. Just when everything seems to be going well, it throws you a curveball—a harsh reminder that nothing is ever truly certain. The same cruel twist that struck me in 1963, when my mother passed away at the young age of 52, came for me again in early 2016. I had retired to bed nursing a mild cold, unaware of the storm about to unfold. In the stillness of the early hours, we were jolted awake by the sound of the phone ringing. It was Jill. Her voice trembled, each word weighted with sorrow, as she tearfully delivered the devastating news that shattered our world. Tracey, our beloved daughter, had been diagnosed with cancer.

What made the moment even more heart-wrenching was that Tracey could not bring herself to tell me. The weight of her diagnosis, the enormity of the battle that loomed ahead, was too heavy for her to voice to her father. In that instant, time seemed to stand still. My heart sank, and the ground beneath me seemed to give way entirely. How could this be? She was so young, so radiant, so full of life and purpose. It seemed unbearably unfair—a cruel blow that defied all reason. All I could think was, "Why her? Why now?"

In the midst of this deeply shocking news, there came a bittersweet piece of joy—Tracey and Nick, after so many years together, had decided to get married. They planned a ceremony for March of that year. Tracey and Nick's decision to marry amid the shadow of her illness was an act of defiant hope—a luminous celebration of love in the face of life's cruel uncertainties. The news filled me with both happiness and a profound sense of sorrow. I was thrilled they had chosen to formalise their commitment, but the shadow of Tracey's illness loomed over the celebration. Sarah, Lina and I flew to Melbourne for the wedding. They were married on March 20, 2016, in a beautiful park surrounded by close family from both sides. It was a joyous occasion, filled with love, laughter and hope, yet there was an unspoken undercurrent, a silent acknowledgement of the battle Tracey was facing. Still, we clung to optimism, trusting that modern medicine would find a way to halt the relentless advance of her illness.

For the rest of 2016 and well into 2017, Tracey endured countless treatments and experimental trials. Hope became a flickering candle, sometimes bright, sometimes dim, but never fully extinguished. For anyone who has witnessed a loved one's fight against cancer, they will understand the anguish of oscillation between hope and despair. It was a relentless rollercoaster. Each promising new treatment would lift our spirits, only to have our hopes dashed as it failed. We clung to every piece of good news like a lifeline, only to feel it unravel as the reality of her illness pressed down once more. The emotional toll on the family was exhausting, but what Tracey went through was far beyond anything I could imagine. The treatments were brutal, and the side effects devastating. It was a relentless assault on her body and spirit. And I, as her father, could do nothing but watch and pray, feeling utterly helpless.

Midway through 2017, I returned to Melbourne to help in whatever small ways I could. Jill and Chrissy, Nick's mother, were doing their best to keep the family afloat, but the weight of Tracey's illness had taken its toll on everyone. I stepped into the routine of their daily lives, helping with the children, cooking, cleaning—small acts of care that felt monumental. My role, though small, was a way for me to stay close to Tracey, to support her and her family through this darkest of times.

But despite all the love, prayers and medical care in the world, the cancer was relentless. Slowly, inevitably, Tracey's condition worsened. On the morning of 19 August 19 2017, she took her last breath. Thankfully she was not alone, as her mother, Jill, had moved into the ward to keep vigil through the final hours. There are moments in life where time seems to fracture. This was one of those moments. The room was filled with an almost unbearable weight of shared grief. With me were Jill, Sera, Nick, Nisi and two of Tracey's closest friends (Kat Ellinghaus and Kalissa Alexeyeff) standing together, united in our sorrow. I will never forget the silence that followed, heavy with loss and pain. Even though we had known this moment was coming, the finality of it was shattering. I wanted to hold on to her, to freeze time, to rewrite this cruel reality, to bring Tracey back to life. But I could not.

In the abyss of grief, my faith became the unyielding thread pulling me through, a reminder of life's eternal continuity beyond this transient world. It was like a thread pulling me out of a chasm of despair, reminding me of a reality beyond the pain. Without that belief, I do not know how I would have survived that moment. I found solace in imagining Tracey meeting my parents in the next world. I could almost hear her telling them about her beautiful children, Nisi and Jimmy, and sharing stories of their lives. It was a comforting thought, but it did not take away the searing pain of her absence.

I often turned to the Baha'i prayers for strength. Two prayers in particular, resonated deeply during those dark days. One I mentioned in an earlier chapter:

"Is there any Remover of difficulties save God? Say: Praised be God! He is God! All are His servants, and all abide by His bidding."

The words "All abide by His bidding" in this context are a constant reminder of the glimmer of hope. In a world that felt suddenly devoid of meaning, it reminded me that there was still a higher purpose at work, even if it was beyond my understanding. This prayer for the departed also offered profound comfort:

"O my God! O thou forgiver of sins, bestower of gifts, dispeller of afflictions! Verily, I beseech Thee to forgive the sins of such as have abandoned the physical garment and have ascended the spiritual world. O my Lord! Purify them from trespasses, dispel their sorrows, and change their darkness into light. Cause them to enter the garden of happiness, cleanse them with the most pure water, and grant them to behold Thy splendours on the loftiest mount."

These words were like a gentle balm to my spirit, soothing the ache of losing her, carrying me through the long nights of grief when sleep was elusive, providing a steady foundation in the face of overwhelming loss. The memories of Tracey's laughter, warmth and her resolute determination played endlessly in my mind.

As a measure of the high regard the university had for Tracey, and in consultation with the family, they established the **Tracey Banivanua Mar Scholarship**. La Trobe University's creation of this scholarship stands as a living testament to her life's work—empowering Pacific Islanders and First Nations Australian students in humanities and social sciences, carrying forward her legacy of advocacy and excellence. It is an honour that continues to inspire us. Today, as I sit writing this memoir, I received news from the university of its latest recipient, a moment that fills me with immense pride, especially knowing how deeply Tracey valued her heritage.

Losing your child is a pain unlike any other. It is a wound that never truly heals. And yet, as I write this, I hold on to the belief that she is in a better place, free from pain, surrounded by the love of those who have gone before. I imagine her smile, radiant and unencumbered, her spirit soaring beyond the limitations of this earthly world. It gives me the strength to keep going, to honour her memory in whatever way I can. For me, her loss defies words—a heartbreak that carves an unfillable void, yet within that void lies the enduring echoes of love, laughter and the continuing essence of who she was.

CHAPTER 31

A JOURNEY CONTINUES

As I sit here in the autumn of 2024, reflecting on the tapestry of my life, it is both remarkable and humbling to see how the threads have woven themselves into patterns unexpected and beautiful. Memories rise and fall like waves, some sharp and vivid, others soft and distant, but all connected by the unrelenting tide of time. Emotions remain raw as if they were only yesterday, yet there is also a sense of calm—of a journey that, while not yet over, has reached a place of contentment.

Our home in Cheltenham has become more than a dwelling; it is a haven. England rich in history, tradition and resilience, with its rolling downs, rugged coastlines, misty moors, and quiet rivers, has been both a sanctuary and an endless source of discovery. Those early seven-day walking holidays with Sarah exploring the hidden corners of this land remain some of my fondest memories. Each footstep revealed something new—a wildflower here, a hidden village there, the scent of damp earth and the whisper of the wind. Those walks were not just about exploring a place; they were about grounding ourselves, discovering each other, and weaving deeper bonds of love and understanding. I often joked with Sarah, "Why would you ever need to travel elsewhere when there is so much right here?"

It was said with a smile, but there was truth in it. There is a simple beauty in discovering the depth of one place, in feeling the land beneath your feet as if it were an extension of yourself.

And yet, the journey was never just about a place; it has always been about the people who filled it.

Family, our greatest treasure

Family—the enduring anchor through life's tempests and calm seas—remains life's greatest treasure, binding us through generations with love and shared purpose.

Now, all my siblings have come and gone, each leaving behind their own legacy.

- Kata, the eldest, who married Qalo from our village, became the headman—a testament to the unwavering confidence the village chief and elders had in his wisdom, work ethic and inclusivity.
- Sera, my beloved sister and the second eldest, married the island chief Ratu Nacanieli Draunidalo. She emerged as the formidable family matriarch whose relentless drive to secure educational opportunities for her siblings was deeply appreciated.
- Jone, the third eldest and the brother I had never met until that self-initiated adventure to Vatukoula when I was just twelve. He returned to our village, married Biu, and became a steadfast pillar among the church elders.
- Biu, the fourth eldest, who sadly passed away young, remains a figure I remember only in stories.
- George, the fifth eldest, who married Ani—my favourite sister-in-law—was my guide and role model

during my teenage years. He was strong as our family leader when our elder siblings passed away, always steady and dependable.

- Sisi, my cherished sister and the sixth eldest, exceptionally bright but, constrained by tradition, was denied further education. We were inseparable in our youth, sharing dreams and burdens side by side. She married Suli from Kadavu, one of life's true gentlemen.

- Tevita, my younger brother, was a man of strong convictions and deep religious faith. He married Bale from our village and went on to become a theological scholar and the President of the Uniting Church of Fiji and Rotuma.

- And then there was Cakacaka, the youngest and the ninth who married Lawedua from the island of Totoya. Brilliant but occasionally rebellious like me, he dedicated his life to education, serving as a headteacher in several primary schools before his untimely passing.

Finally, there is me, the seventh child—still here to put all of this down on paper as a memoir, a remembrance of my journey and a glimmer into my family's history. Writing these words feels like stitching together fragments— fragments of deep sorrow and hilarity, but mostly fulfilment, happiness and family. Each piece represents a life lived fully, a bond cherished, and a story worth telling.

Now, Sera and Ben are raising their own young family in Victoria, Australia. They have found their calling in the Australian Defence Forces, with their child embracing their unique paths. Monty—whom I fondly call Yaca— nurtures his musical talents with the Australian Children's

Choir and his beloved keyboard, and Sera has become a loving responsible mother reminiscent of her namesake, my sister Sera. Some of her wonderful artistic talent and joie de vivre comes through in her photographic work.

Tracey, though absent, lives on in the vibrant spirits of her children. Nisi, much like her mother, is captivated by history and books, while Jimmy remains the unstoppable force of energy we have always known. I imagine Tracey's pride as she watches from the spiritual realm, her spirit and love echoing through the lives of her children.

Meanwhile, Lina has carved out a fulfilling life in London, working for the BBC, yet she remains ever connected to home. Whether it is visiting for one of Sarah's home-cooked meals or discussing the latest world events, her presence is a source of joy. Lina's adventurous spirit and keen intellect remind me of the boundless possibilities life offers, even amid its challenges. That indomitable sense of adventure continues to shine through, sometimes with unexpected consequences—like her recent ACL injury while playing touch rugby with her team!

Beyond her resilience and zest for life, Lina has grown into a woman of remarkable strength and quiet leadership. Both Sarah and I have come to trust her implicitly with important family decisions. In her calm yet decisive way, she has become the steady bridge that binds us all, connecting the past, present and future of our family with grace and unending love.

And then, there is Sarah... my steadfast partner, my rock. She has been my steadying compass, pointing me towards hope even in the darkest storms. She is the love of my life who has journeyed with me through trials and triumphs, through loss and love. We have faced the unknown together—from the bustling chaos of Port

Moresby to the serene calm of Cheltenham, from the tumult of coups in Fiji to the quiet of English gardens. We have weathered storms and, through it all, her untiring support has been my anchor, her love the guiding star that illuminates even the darkest paths.

Reflections and gratitude

The years have not been without their challenges. We have endured family tragedies, the grief of saying goodbye to those we loved too soon, and the turbulence of a world that changes faster than we can keep up. The Covid pandemic was yet another chapter—a time of isolation, but also a time for deep reflection. In those still moments, I often found myself pondering not what I had achieved, but who I had become. Yet, here we are, on the other side, perhaps a bit older, a bit greyer, but undoubtedly stronger.

We do not often celebrate birthdays as adults, but there are exceptions. Sarah's 70th birthday was one of those special moments. After the long shadow of Covid, it felt like a burst of sunlight breaking through the clouds. It was not just a celebration of her years but a tribute to her unwavering light in our lives. It was a chance for me to express my deep appreciation once again for standing by me, for being the steady hand through all the highs and lows.

And soon, it will be my turn. Next year, I will reach my 80th birthday—a milestone I once could not have imagined. It will be a celebration not of age, but of endurance, love and the countless hands that have lifted me along the way.

As I close this chapter, I find myself at a new juncture—not an ending, but rather a continuation.

Life is a river, ever flowing, carving new paths even as it carries echoes of the past. There are still gardens to plant or visit, books to read, grandchildren to watch grow up and more walks to take with Sarah by my side.

My life has been a mosaic of different and diverse cultures, places and experiences—from the sun-drenched beaches of Fiji to the cold, snowy mornings of England. But the most profound lessons were not learned in boardrooms or even during political upheavals. They were found in the simple moments: the laughter of my children and grandchildren, the steady presence of my wife and the quiet strength of faith—a legacy built not on ambition, but on love and service.

For now, this is where my story pauses. The journey continues, but it is no longer mine alone. It belongs to my children, my grandchildren and those who will come after. I have done my part; now, it is their turn to write their own chapters.

In the end, what matters most is not the achievements, promotions or accolades, but the people we touch, the love we give, the lives we help shape and the legacies we leave behind. The echoes of kindness resonate far longer than the applause of success.

EPILOGUE

Though this memoir ends, the story, like life itself, goes on. Here is to the next chapter, whatever it may bring, and to the grace that has carried me this far.

www.ingramcontent.com/pod-product-compliance
Lightning Source LLC
LaVergne TN
LVHW011156080426
835508LV00007B/433